THE EXAMPLE

SETTING THE STANDARD FOR YOURSELF AND OTHERS

RYAN STEWMAN

REASONS TO READ THIS BOOK ...

"Ryan Stewman is direct and right to the point. The principles he teaches will take your company to the next level! Love this dude!"

Bridger Pennington — Founder, Investment Fund Secrets

"Without integrity, nothing in life works, which is why I often say that integrity is my love language. Ryan is the total embodiment of integrity. He 100% shows up in every single way in his life: for his family, in his business, in what he says he is going to do, and when he says he is going to do it. This is why he succeeds. On top of it all, he has a heart of gold. That is why he is an inspiration and the example that we should ALL be following."

Rebecca Zung — TV Host, YouTube Personality, Attorney

"Ryan is one of the hardest working men I know. He's passionate about people living their best lives now and an expert at giving them the tools to do so. He's an amazing family man and friend. I'm honored to call him brother."

David J. Harris Jr. — Political Influencer

"Ryan speaks on leadership and leads a fantastic coaching organization. He talks about the value of family and leads his family with faith and love. Ryan truly exemplifies what he teaches."

Brian McKittrick — Director of Sales, Insurance of Texas

"Ryan is a rare cat indeed. He knows that winning involves making everyone else around him better. He can get people to extract their very best effort even if it's hidden from themselves."

Antonio Swad — Founder, Wingstop Restaurants

"Stewman is the example of what's possible through the power of thought, intention, and execution."

Steve Jordan - Navy SEAL & Apex Elite Performance Coach

"People rarely listen to what they are told to do. But they often imitate the actions of those they see around them (good and bad). If you want to be a leader and have massive influence and impact people's lives, you have to master the art of becoming an example, and Ryan Stewman has done just that. This book is a must-read if you want to expand your influence and impact as many lives as possible by becoming your own version of The Example!"

Shawn Sharma — 8-Figure Serial Entrepreneur

"As one of the old guys in the room, if you really want to be the best version of yourself, you can't wait around, hitch up to Ryan NOW, and get ready to be the best you can be in every aspect of life!!!"

Sammie Knight — Multi-Industry Entrepreneur and Executive Coach

"Ryan is more than an example to me. He lives his life through action, and it leaves an imprint on others and myself. His word is as good as gold, and he always gives more than he receives. Sound like BS? Probably because not many people can actually deliver. Ryan ALWAYS OVER delivers! I'm writing this from an island in Italy. Without Ryan and his team, my family dream vacation would not be possible! Congratulations on your new book!"

Patrick Bolanos — Co-Owner, Trailer King Builders

"The reason Ryan continues to win is that he adds an incredible amount of value to people's lives. Every day he is on social media teaching and sharing and helping human beings become better."

Sean Whalen — Founder, Lions Not Sheep

"EXAMPLE: I always knew I was here for a reason. Always had drive and perseverance, but working with Ryan Stewman in the last two years, I have realized that it is my duty to become a better leader for those individuals around us. As Ryan says, 'FYE.' That meaning stuck with me and made me realize that I had to become a better version of myself in every situation in my life, meaning my spirituality, my family, and my community. He has taught me how to level up like nobody has ever taught me before. With a leveling up of myself constantly, I am able to give back to individuals that need my service. By filling my cup, I am able to fill multiple other people's cups up, as well. Hands-down, I am blessed to be able to be within Ryan's community and brotherhood."

Jennifer Carrasco — EOS Business Coach

"Ryan is a phenomenal coach and mentor. Within 18 months of working with him, I learned growth strategies that allowed me to launch two best-selling books, speak on stage in front of thousands of people, get verified on social media, and land features in top publications like Forbes. Being a part of his community is a game changer."

Jessica Dennehy — CEO, Pivot & Slay

"Ryan was the first leader outside special operations that changed my life. Great culture WILL change lives, and great leaders MUST create that culture. He leads by example, he does the work, and he gives first. Following strong leaders into battle is underrated—there is no better recipe for success."

Zack Hughes — Green Beret & Apex Elite Performance Coach

"Ryan is the exception, and we are all better for it because of his tenacity and passion. He is everything he says he is, does, and believes."

Brenda Neckvatal — The Drone Biz Coach

"Stewman is relentless in a good way!"

Dan Young — Founder of PC Laptops

"I have read every single book that Ryan Stewman has ever put in front of me. Each one of them is amazing, and this one is no different. All of these books read like adventure novels that happen to be 100% true. What's great about them is that not only are they the types of books that are impossible to stop reading, but you also learn something on every single page. It helps that the books are also absolutely hilarious. I recommend this book to everybody, and I'm 100% certain that you will find it extremely valuable and that you will be just as glad to have read it as I am."

Frank Kern — Internet Marketing's OG Homeboy

"Ryan invested his time putting in the work and building relationships. He shows you the 'how' and 'what' so you can produce the most elite version of the 'why' in your life."

Danny Galvez — Founder, Voice Your Life Media

"Ryan Stewman has never ceased to amaze me. The dude came from the bottom—technically below the bottom—yet through all that adversity, he has produced millions for himself and countless others."

Brad Lea — Founder, LightSpeed VT

"Stewman is truly one of the real ones. He lives his truth every day. He leads from the front and provides everyone a blueprint on how to dominate in business and life despite your past."

Jeff Fenster — Founder, Everbowl

"Ryan is the most authentic person I know who has a powerful way of motivating and teaching incredible life and business lessons. He's an incredible marketing and sales mind who is always providing value."

Dusty Black — Country Music Artist and Founder of Black Tie Moving

"Ryan Stewman has been one of my all-time favorite people to do biz with. Ryan, above anyone else I've met, does exactly what he says he will do! Always over delivers!"

Aaron Wagner — CEO, Wags Capital

"Success leaves clues, and Ryan exemplifies this principle!"

Burton P. Hughes — *USA Today and Wall Street Journal* Best-Selling Author

GET IN TOUCH

SOCIAL MEDIA

Facebook: 339,000 Followers

> Fan: www.Facebook.com/HardcoreCloser
> STWSP Group: www.Facebook.com/groups/salestalk
> Personal: www.Facebook.com/RealRyanStewman

Twitter: 15,000 Followers

> Personal: www.Twitter.com/RyanStewman
> Business: www.Twitter.com/HardcoreCloser

LinkedIn: 17,000 Followers

> Personal: www.LinkedIn.com/in/RyanStewman/
> Business: www.linkedin.com/company/Hardcore-Closer/

Instagram: 278,000 Followers

> Business: www.Instagram.com/HardcoreCloser

TikTok: 110,000 Followers

> Personal: www.TikTok.com/@hardcorecloser

YouTube: 8.8 Million Views/ 22 Million Minutes Watched

> Business: www.YouTube.com/c/RyanStewmanOfficial

PODCASTS

> *THC Podcast*
> Top 50 Business Podcast on iTunes, 1.3M Listeners

> *Rewire Podcast*
> Top 50 Business Podcast on iTunes, 3.4M Listeners

BEST SELLING BOOKS

GCode: How to Stay Super Focused in a World Full of Distractions (2020)

Social Media Millions: Your Guide to Making Massive Amounts of Money from Social Media Selling (2018)

M3: Media Marketing Method (2018)

*F*ck Your Excuses: The Misfit's Guide to Avoiding Upper Limits (2018)*

Sell Your Ass Off: How to Make the Most of a Sales Job in the Marketplace (2018)

Sell It and Scale It: How to Transition from Salesman to CEO (2018)

Elevator to the Top: Your Go-To Resource for All Things Sales (2016)

Kick Ass: Take Names, Emails, and Phone Numbers (2016)

Bulletproof Business: Protect Yourself Against the Competition (2016)

Hardcore [c]loser, A Top Business Book of All Time (2015)

WEBSITES

Hardcore Closer Blog

  www.HardcoreCloser.com
  Articles. Digital Products. Training Resources.

Break Free Academy

  www.BreakFreeAcademy.com

Phonesites

  www.Phonesites.com

TABLE OF CONTENTS

FOREWORD

You're holding in your hand a life-changing book.

Ryan Stewman is the extreme example of what a person should be and look like. I am proud and honored to say that he is the prime example of what each of us should strive to be like.

Here's a little bit about myself to help you appreciate why I feel so strongly about Ryan being an example to many.

As an individual, I have made countless mistakes that have taught me great lessons. One lesson has been the importance of surrounding yourself with individuals who walk the walk and have character, integrity, and more.

I left school in the 9th grade, and through many failures in business, I figured out the basic formula that most know. At the time, I choose to ignore it.

I went on to start a company with zero dollars and eventually sell it for one billion dollars. During that journey, I compounded many investments, including a $750 million multifamily real estate portfolio.

I am not telling you this to impress you but to illustrate that none of this would have been possible had I not exposed myself to individuals who "walk the walk," just like Ryan does.

Living this way has enabled me to scale in my businesses and life. If I had not involved myself with the "Ryan Stewmans" of the world, living the bona fide results of their hard-earned efforts despite a river of mistakes, I would not be financially free today.

Our friendship started when I met Ryan through mutual acquaintances. To say the least, he was an interesting individual and obviously successful, but I was intrigued to know more about him. Did he have a family? If so, how was he as a husband, father, leader, and so on?

As Ryan and I got to know each other through mutual investments, seeing one another at speaking events, and so forth, slowly but surely, I learned who the real Ryan was—the one I didn't know yet. The more our casual business relationship grew, the more I was overly impressed with his business sense, especially in the technology space, which would shock most... Let's just say he's definitely a nerd (and I mean this in the kindest way). Don't let the tattoos and tough demeanor fool you. Many think my come-up is a crazy American dream story, but now that I know Ryan, he's the prime example of how someone should "walk the walk" to get where they want to go.

I see how he is as a husband, father, and leader to his companies. His drive to create a better future for generations to come impresses me every day. Ryan and I now frequently communicate on a personal and business basis, so I know why he is successful in business and outside of business.

I'm overly proud of Ryan. Not only because of his business success but more so because of his constant growth.

The Example is a powerful book. It is made even more so by understanding that the author is an individual who has accomplished incredible feats, incredible positive financial outcomes, and incredible life circumstances.

Take it from this serial entrepreneur, who has accomplished financial freedom yet constantly thrives for more. This book is a game-changer for anyone who truly wants unthinkable outcomes for themselves and their family.

Cheers to you, Ryan, and may life continue shining a bright light on you and your family, as well as the thousands of people you impact daily. You are an example of what this great country offers to each and every one of us.

Your friend,

Bobby Castro
Founder of Bankers Health Group and Venture Capitalist

A QUICK HEADS UP

You might be reading this book wondering who I am or why I would consider myself the example. Or you might not know who I am and think I have a lot of audacity to write a book about being the example.

Let's start at the beginning.

This book isn't about me and everything I've done. Yes, I'll tell you stories that involve myself, but that's not where I want you to focus. This book is about us as a whole.

This book, the lessons inside it, and the inspirations I am providing are far beyond anything I could be an example of. I can only be a part of what we are striving for together. The whole of this is larger than anything I can lead. When it comes to this mission, I can't do it alone. I am asking you to do it with me.

We need more people who are examples in the world. As you continue reading, I want you to become inspired enough that you will go on to become the example for others around you.

No matter at what point in history you're reading this book, whether a thousand years in the future or tomorrow, the undeniable fact is that the world needs more examples.

The world needs more leaders who can step up and show people what integrity, responsibility, and owning our mistakes and learning from them look like.

The world needs more of us.

The world doesn't need more perfect people or people who pretend to be perfect.

The world needs more examples.

The world needs more men and women who've shined their light through the darkness.

The world needs more men and women who've gone through the pits of hell but now have a heavenly life.

The world needs more examples of what's possible when you are willing to do the work.

I didn't write this book to become a best seller or get words off my chest or out of my mind. I wrote it to motivate you to become the example for those around you.

If you lead yourself, teach yourself and be the example for yourself, you'll also become the example for others.

In a world without standards, where there is more of an extreme lack of examples than anything else, you can stand out in high demand amid low supply. That means you get to be a person of value. That value comes from you being the example.

This book will lay out exactly how you can become the example for your family, friends, employees, coworkers, everybody around you, and yourself. You'll even be seen as the example in the eyes of random people in public.

Most importantly, you get to be the example.

So don't just read this book.

Live and breathe it in because the rest of the planet needs you to be the example.

We need you to show others what's possible. That's how we change the world for the better.

Rise above,
Ryan Stewman

PART 1:
LIFE WITHOUT DESIGN

CHAPTER 1

LIFE WITHOUT STANDARDS

"How will you know what you stand for
if you haven't clearly defined your standards?"

I don't know about you, but I grew up in a household with rules and no real standards. My parents had rules for everything: what time we kids could eat, how much we could eat, what time we went to bed, when we took a shower, when we took a bath, when we went to school, when we went to work, and so on.

They had rules based around our entire life, but we didn't have any standards.

By standards, I mean the qualities we use to measure our lives. As young people, we don't know to look for standards. We just know how to abide by rules. This lack of standards doesn't make our parents bad people—because they didn't know any better. As I'm writing this, I'm in my 40s. My parents are in their 60s. I know now that they didn't have access to the information we do now. No one even thought about doing anything different other than setting the rules and making sure they were followed.

MISUNDERSTANDING STANDARDS

Subconsciously everybody—including our parents—has standards. But in many cases, our parents didn't know to identify them as standards, so they classified them as rules.

Think about the mental implications of growing up like that. We were ruled over instead of maturing with standards. We had to follow our parents' rules, but because they couldn't get in touch with their standards buried deep in their subconscious, life was black and white: you were either a rule breaker or a rule keeper.

I know now that when you change your life and your children's life from one that's designed and dictated by rules to one with set standards, things change.

MY FAMILY'S STANDARDS

In my household today, just like in everybody else's, we have a few rules. If you have kids, you need rules, of course. The difference is that we have positioned ourselves to have standards as a family.

For example, it's not a rule that you push your chair in when you get up from the table. It's the standard that we set for being a Stewman. We do the work, and one of our family's core values and a part of doing that work includes pushing in your chair. It's not a rule that you shut the door behind you when you come in and out of the house. It's a standard that we don't leave the door open in the house. It's not a rule that you have to turn your light switch off in the Stewman household. It's a standard that we don't waste money—therefore, we don't waste electricity that *costs* money. As my kids grow up, they will have high standards instead of being highly ruled over.

Again, because our parents didn't have the information or opportunity to understand and implement standards, it doesn't make them bad. It doesn't make them anything other than lacking in information.

You can live a different life with your family, too. And after you read this book, you will have the opportunity to set standards because you will know better.

SOCIETY'S LACK OF STANDARDS

Society doesn't set standards.

The government doesn't set standards for American success, either. They pass rules to lord over us. Worse yet, society's standards are steadily decreasing.

School standards are at an all-time low. A 2021 news article states that all schools within the University of California system will no longer require the ACT or SAT as an admissions requirement. These school standards used to be measured by these tests. The minimum SAT score to attend a college in the US ranges between 950-1050. It's common knowledge that if you score 1600, you are pretty much a genius and can go anywhere you want. So why take that away?[1]

In essence, schools in that system are giving the message: "These tests are no longer a standard. As long as you show up, we're going to pass you."

This incident, among many others, is our call to action.

When society lowers its standards, we need to raise ours.

When the rest of the world is enamored with behaving in a way that reflects lower standards, don't just jump in and follow them. Take a deep look at what people are doing. If it seems out of alignment with your best self, figure out why you shouldn't do what they're doing. Make a different decision.

Warren Buffet said it best: "Be greedy when people are fearful, and fearful when people are greedy." If the world's adapting to and chasing subpar standards to lower the level of performance needed to reach a goal, don't

---

[1] https://www.cbs8.com/article/news/local/california/university-of-california-system-act-sat-scores/509-b9064af3-73f2-41c7-802b-773613e1d30a

follow their lead. Be the person setting high standards for yourself. Don't follow everyone else mindlessly and apply their low standards to yourself.

SETTING RELATIONSHIP STANDARDS

In relationships, people often don't set any or many standards, either.

Most of my friends are married now, but when I was younger, they would say stuff like, "Dude, I'll bang anything," and "She's got a nice butt. I'll go out with her." My friends didn't have any standards at the time. But inevitably, they would get together with a girl they hadn't put much thought into, and after some time, and the relationship crumbling, they would wonder why it hadn't worked.

They couldn't understand what was wrong and would argue their points: "We're spending time together. We live together. We go out on dates. We sleep together but are not getting any further in this relationship." Of course, they weren't. They hadn't set any standards. Their level of acceptance was shallow. These low standards revolved around the basest of human emotions between two people: "Oh, you like me? I like you. This should work out. Let's try it."

My wife, Amy, is a woman of high standards. I happen to be a great salesperson. But she taught me to have standards for myself.

Growing up poor, not having anything, and going through the hardships and setbacks I've dealt with in my life didn't teach me standards. I was used to being ruled over and had no idea how having high standards could change my life. Any standards I may have had were low. Then I met Amy, and that all changed. I learned to have high standards for myself.

One of the standards that Amy and I set in our relationship is to stay in shape. We have promised to work out and be good-looking for life. There will not be a point in our relationship when we say to each other, "You no longer have to go to the gym. You no longer have to eat healthily. It's okay for us just to be fat and happy or fat and unhealthy."

No, no, no.

We set standards for our fitness. I go to the gym every day at 5:00 AM, Monday through Friday. That's my commitment to her: "I'm going to be there for you, babe. I'm doing this for you, the kids, and me. When I married you, I looked like this. I want to stay married to you looking like this."

When people get into a relationship, they often have standards in the beginning, then they slowly let themselves and their standards go.

Look around, and you'll notice that everybody's committed to living without standards. That might be normal and okay in today's society, but it's not okay for me, and it shouldn't be okay for you.

A couple of generations ago, schools had high standards and put out better-quality people like our grandparents. These people were very accountable and responsible. They took extreme ownership of anything they did. They were hard workers. Many of our parents—if they were from that era—were the same. Grandparents stayed married for life. My grandparents got married when they were sixteen. They're in their 90s today and still married!

The continual lowering of standards in society has created people like me—before I got it together. I lived a life without standards. I was divorced three times. Thankfully, I've never had a problem with my fitness standards, but some people have to buy two seats on a plane. I don't want that to be me, and it never will be.

STANDARDS TO ELEVATE YOUR LIFE

Think about what standards are missing that you need to set in your life. Don't consider what rules or values you live by. Go deeper. Ask yourself: *what standards am I not willing to lower?*

What you do with the answer to this question is where change starts and sticks.

That answer will dictate the direction of the rest of your life. Up until this point, you may have lived a life without standards, but today, at this moment, that changes.

From this point forward, you will set new standards for yourself.

What's your physical standard?

What's your mental standard?

What's your relationship standard?

What's your financial standard?

Once you get this foundation down and understand and set your new standards, the direction of your life will be forever changed—as long as you abide by these changes.

Before you move on to the next chapter, set some fresh standards for yourself. Write down the list above. Then rewrite your physical, mental, relationship, and financial standards.

For instance, a new mental standard might be: "I'm going to read x number of books per month." Or "I'm going to practice meditation every day."

My mental standard is reading no less than ten pages per day. To meet my physical standard, I go to the gym every day and keep to a diet. My financial standard revolves around how many hours I will put in at work and understanding how much money that means for me. I will not do anything less than this, and I will make sure I abide by these standards— just like I asked you to do. You will define your own standards and stick to them daily, too.

Lastly, I have very high standards around the people I let in my life. I refuse to let substandard folks close to me. My standards allow me only to have a certain pedigree of people in my circle. This standard doesn't mean you can shit on somebody else. It means the people around you will rise to your standards and continue to be a part of your life, or they will make a conscious decision not to be the example for themselves. In these cases, they usually show themselves out.

True integrity means adhering to the standards you set. It means sticking to them even when it's hard—especially when it's hard.

You wouldn't be reading this book if you didn't want standards and deserve them.

So take the time to write them down, and make sure that you live and abide by these new ways of life because when it comes to being the change you want to see, your commitment to these new standards matters.

CHAPTER 2

THE WRONG EXAMPLE

"You become who you look up to.
If you look up to no one, you become a no one."

Before I go on about the examples I've set for myself, I have to be transparent and tell you the truth of who I am—or was.

For most of my life, I've been the *wrong* example.

I was somebody you didn't want to model.

I was somebody you would never trade places with.

People thought of me as an example of nothing but failure. I was a walking, living, breathing example of failure.

It's crazy to even think back on that time now. Our mission at the companies I run and own—including Apex, our mastermind network—is to represent what winning looks like at all times.

My life used to be the exact opposite of winning. Yes, I've lost it all—a few times. But as they say:

"You're not a real hustler until you've lost it all and got it back."

If that theory is true, I'm one hell of a hustler because that's the pattern I lived for a long time.

I get it. And maybe now you're thinking, why would I want to take advice from somebody who used to be an example of failure, an example of what not to do?

There's a very good reason.

Wisdom comes from learning from your mistakes. I have spent 30 years of my life as a prolific mistake maker, surrounded by prolific mistake makers. It was in choosing to learn from my mistakes and the mistakes of those around me that I became one of the wisest men among men. It might have taken me 30 years, but I got there.

Einstein said, "Insanity is doing the same thing over and over and expecting different results." I say, "An idiot is a person who makes the same mistake over and over again, expecting different results."

I didn't make the same mistake a million times. I made a million mistakes once, but each took me closer to wisdom.

Each mistake came with a lesson.

Each mistake was a blessing in disguise, but I didn't know that. I just assumed I was the wrong example.

Maybe you're assuming that right now too. Listen, whatever dark past you're hiding from, it can't be any worse than mine.

INTRODUCING RYAN RUSSELL MCCORD

Let me tell you a story about a guy named Ryan Russell McCord. He was born at the end of the 70s, right before the turn of a new decade, in the dawn of neon and thigh-high socks.

Ryan McCord was born into an upper-middle-class family that owned a horse farm. His father was a champion horse rider. His mother was the daughter of a banker. Ryan's grandparents owned banks and businesses throughout rural Texas.

In the mid-80s, a company called The Resolution Trust Company bought out all the Savings & Loans (S&Ls) and caused the market to crash. Ryan McCord's grandparents lost their businesses and their banks. When Ryan McCord's parents split, his dad disappeared from his life. His mom moved to a new city and married a man who adopted Ryan. This new stepfather also liked to beat the shit out of Ryan and put him to work.

At age seven, Ryan Russell McCord became Ryan Keith Stewman. At age 15, Ryan Stewman dropped out of high school to work at a local car wash for his stepfather. One day, Ryan's stepfather chased him up the stairs into his bedroom. At that time, Ryan was 16 and weighed 130 pounds. His stepfather weighed 250 pounds. Scared for his life, Ryan jumped out the window.

You know, obviously, that young man was me. As I look back on that incident, I vividly remember that I promised myself, *"This is the last time that motherfucker ever hits me."* I broke my wrist in the fall but was scared to go to the hospital. We didn't have insurance. Long story short, I now have zero movement in my right wrist. If you're keeping track: I was adopted and fatherless, had dropped out of school, and had a broken arm and a massive amount of pain—all by the age of sixteen.

Once I jumped out that window, I didn't go back home. I ran the streets. The first business opportunity was selling drugs. Drugs led to getting in trouble with the police, and that eventually led to prison.

In prison, I decided to get my life together. I served my time and was paroled successfully. Then I went back to work for my stepfather at the car wash and decided to become the best car washer on the planet. Eventually, that standard earned me a job in the mortgage business.

That's when my life changed.

For the first time, I started making money, went to church, and even got married. Within six months of being married, the woman I married hit herself in the head with a pan, called the police and said I did it. Despite not having phone cameras back then to prove my case, I won in court. The battle and subsequent divorce drained all my money, my energy, and my soul.

But life was about to get worse.

When I finally got my life back together, I remarried and successfully built a mortgage business. I did so well that the cops raided my house thinking I was selling drugs again. I wasn't doing anything but working hard. They still sent me to prison for a crime I didn't commit.

While locked up, my second wife divorced me and left me for our land-scaper. Now, I was a two-time divorcee and prison inmate. I had no leadership. I had nothing but conditional love. The women in my life loved me if I had money. My family loved me if I didn't cause problems. They didn't want to help me anytime I got into trouble. No, they avoided me.

I got out of prison the second time and reentered the mortgage business, working as hard as possible. Oh, by the way, it was the worst time to do mortgages, circa 2008-2010. That didn't matter; I was still cranking out loans. In July 2010, Congress passed the Dodd-Frank Wall Street Reform and Consumer Protection Act, restricting felons from holding mortgage licenses. Suddenly, I couldn't do mortgages anymore and didn't know what to do. All I could think was *I don't have a job. I don't have anything.*

That's when I tried network marketing. I made some money, but the company I was with switched the comp plan on me. I took a serious cut in my commission. To get back on my feet, I learned about internet marketing and started running ads for Ryan Deiss' e-book, *Continuity Blueprint,* which taught me how to set up a WordPress site. His book inspired me to buy another e-book by Frank Kern, called *List Control,* which ironically instructed people on how to write an e-book. That was the beginning of my author career. I wrote *Know What You're Owed* to protect homebuyers from a scam in the industry at the time. If someone bought a new house, the lender would swindle them into making a higher payment because the unscrupulous builder had passed off paying a year's worth of taxes to the customer—leaving them with a larger tax bill. This let the builders pocket more money without the buyer knowing what was happening.

Slowly, I started earning money from the books and ads. In one month, I made $10,000, and the next, I made $20,000. That was the sign I needed of what to do.

I took my life savings and bet on ads. Just like that, one month later, I made $100,000. Then, ten days later, I started getting chargebacks: bing, bing, bing echoed from my computer. That was the sound of people wanting their money back.

All the work I had done to let people know what was going on with the tax swindle wasn't accurate anymore. When the Dodd-Frank Act was passed, people could no longer get away with it. But I wasn't aware of that new information because I wasn't a loan officer anymore.

It was another big hit.

I lost my life savings and the advertisement money. By that time, I was married for the third time and had a kid. I had to borrow money, move in with my in-laws, and sell our house just to cover the bills. That lesson early in my life forced me to come face to face with whether or not I had integrity. I could have easily told all those clients that I wouldn't give them a refund. Instead, I paid back every person who asked me, even though it forced me to rock bottom again.

I felt these clients didn't know any better, and I certainly didn't mean to mislead them. It was only right that I gave them their money back. And guess what? Those refunds were about 10 bucks a pop! Refunding them wasn't going to change their life, but it changed mine. I saw the chance to take the shortcut, but I did the right thing.

Selling the house and moving in with my in-laws stressed out my third marriage. Before long, my wife left. My life now had the additions of a kid and a baby mama.

When I said I was a prolific mistake maker, I just gave you the Cliffs Notes.

I didn't grow up with leadership.

I didn't grow up with examples.

I didn't grow up with standards.

Now that I've set them, I have examples for my life.

I have standards for my life.

I tell you this not so you pity me. My life's amazing now. I want you to see that no matter where you've been in life or how low you've felt, I've probably had it worse and done it worse. If I get to enjoy a good life today, then you can, too. If I get to be an example and set standards, then you can, too. Your standards should be better than mine.

CHAPTER 3

3Ls: LONELY AND LACKING LEADERSHIP

"Everything rises and falls on leadership."

Right now, things in the world are crazier than ever. People are demanding statues of heroes be torn down and statues of criminals erected in their place. Let me be clear; this isn't a book on politics or social-economic debate, but the truth is, we've seen this happen. Not all statues of heroes were removed, and not all statues of criminals were erected.

The media, the government, and the people against folks like you and me are propping up examples and trying to push their party leaders as good people, but they aren't. You and I both know that.

We can't deny that in 2020, citizens in this country took up rioting and protesting for someone who was breaking the law. Every day, people who don't read books like this are being drawn into false narratives suggesting these folks are examples for us to follow. This is not true. Understand right now; there's a dark game being played for your intelligence, your thoughts, your loyalty, and your wisdom.

The truth is, right now, no matter what country you live in,
chances are you're lonely and looking for leadership.
This is the trifecta of the three Ls.

DEFINING THE THREE LS

When you think about who's an example for you, who comes to mind? When I ask, "Who's an example of integrity?" What face do you picture? A long time ago, Abraham Lincoln was one of the greatest examples of a man with integrity. That's how he got the nickname Honest Abe.

Lincoln was a great example. Let's now talk about the present. I challenge you to think about someone living and breathing today who's a standard of honesty for you. Who embodies the physical fitness you admire? Who's a financially ethical person who doesn't cut corners, steal, or cheat?

We've all seen *The Social Network* movie, detailing how Mark Zuckerberg stole the idea for Facebook from the Winklevoss twins. That story's so true that the Winklevoss twins became billionaires off the settlement Mark Zuckerberg gave them a decade ago. Still, we put Zuck up as an example of a tech entrepreneur. In reality, he's an example of dishonesty and thievery. He stole from two other guys and beat them at their own game. When we know the full story, we have to ask ourselves, who are we really looking up to? Who's really the example?[2]

If you thought of somebody who represents integrity, congratulations. If you couldn't think of somebody to fill those shoes, you don't have an example to turn to. It means no one can set your standards for you. It's easy to feel alone in this situation. Maybe you think there's no one you can believe in besides Jesus and yourself. We know Jesus was the truth, and you know yourself—so those answers wouldn't surprise me. If you can't believe in yourself, you're in big trouble. If there's no one to look up to, no one's coming to save us. Without anyone else, you must believe in yourself. You must be the example. If you're the example, you're saving yourself.

[2] https://entrepreneurshandbook.co/the-winklevoss-twins-are-gods-compared-to-mark-zuckerberg-673c4c25898f

That sounds intimidating, I know. You're probably wondering, *how the hell do I do that?* Let me help you out.

When I'm in that position and searching for someone to model myself after, I go to the source of wisdom. If we're going to get anything from life, we first need wisdom.

KING SOLOMON

Let me tell you a story about the richest man who ever lived. His name was King Solomon. He lived back in BC (Before Christ) times. The first recorded events in the Bible originate around this timeline. Solomon was the son of David. Most of us are familiar with the story of David, a shepherd boy who killed the giant Goliath to save the Israelites. David's story is one of persistence against the odds, and so is Solomon's.

Even to this day, Solomon is the richest man who ever lived. He had a multi-trillion-dollar empire—if you're accounting for today's inflation and how money works compared to when he was alive.

Solomon would send convoys of diamonds and gold to trade with other countries like Egypt. He was a baller with a lair of women—hundreds of chicks at his demand. Solomon had it all. He got his riches and awesome life when God came to him and said, "I will give you anything you want. You've been a great servant. Your father has done me well. Go ahead and ask me."

Solomon didn't ask for money. He didn't ask for all those chicks at his beck and call. He didn't ask to be stronger, for a penis enlargement, or any of that stuff.

He asked for wisdom.

RYAN STEWMAN

His plan to conquer all is still relevant today. You need wisdom to be on top—in any area of life.

You want to be fit? Wisdom will give you the knowledge on how to be fit.

You want to be rich? Wisdom will give you both the knowledge of how to be rich and tell you how to apply the action that will give you those results.

You want to get closer to God? Wisdom will teach you how to get closer to God.

You want to build a better relationship with somebody on this planet? Wisdom and knowledge will help you become better at relationships.

**Many pursue wealth for its own sake.
True wealth comes from the pursuit of wisdom.**

In the Book of Proverbs, for instance, wisdom is at the heart and center of moral and intellectual decision-making.

This isn't a religious book. But whether you believe in the Bible or God, you can't prove me wrong on this point. The key to gaining everything is through wisdom. It's not to get money. You want to acquire wisdom, *then* money. You don't want to try and get in good shape first. Learn wisdom, *then* get in good shape.

But how do you attain wisdom?

Wisdom comes from experience. Again, I've made enough mistakes to become wise by not repeating the same mistake. When I avoid making the same mistake, I learn from that experience and gain wisdom.

If you think there's a shortcut to gaining wisdom, there's not. But there is an easier path to take. Don't get me wrong. It's still not easy, but it is worth it. You don't have to read the entire Bible but do read the Book of Proverbs written by King Solomon. Proverbs are sayings of the wise. As I told you, King Solomon was the wisest and the richest man ever to live. He shares his wisdom in the 31 Books of Proverbs (one for each day of the month).

Let's say today's date is April 4th. If I am following a monthly pattern and reading one proverb a day, my proverb of the day is number four, chapter four. It takes about three minutes to read a proverb. The first time you read it, it's confusing. You won't know what the hell this man was talking about. That's the beauty of using the Book of Proverbs as your path to wisdom. Although your first exposure will be confusing, keep at it because a month later, after reading those proverbs for the second time, they will make a little more sense. A month after that, when you read those proverbs for the third time—the meaning will be even clearer.

I've been doing this since 2004, and I'm actively writing this book in 2022. Needless to say, I've read the Book of Proverbs a few times. Every time, I learn something new from it. I gain more wisdom and a deeper understanding of life. I learn once again that wisdom will give me everything I want. When I gain wisdom, I lead myself so others will follow. One of my standards is that I must set the example by being and not saying. This is wisdom.

If I'm going to be the example, I can't say I'm the example and not be it. I have to be the example so people see that I am, then they will share that knowledge with others.

We may not have anybody to look up to. We may not have anybody to save us. We may have had false idols placed in front of us. We may have false sayings spoken in front of us. We may be chasing money instead of chasing wisdom. Allow me to correct that for you. Remember, whether you read Proverbs or not, you can gain wisdom by learning from your mistakes. But consistently reading Proverbs will make getting there easier.

When you have wisdom, you can lead yourself. When you lead yourself, you become an example in your own life; you inspire yourself. When you become an example for yourself, you become an example for others. People become good leaders when they represent good examples for themselves and others. The butterfly effect is exponential. In other words, small incremental changes can lead to significant outcomes. That's why the world needs us—we are part of those changes that affect lives we don't even know about.

Before we start on the next chapter, I want you to hear what I am about to say and believe it. I will keep driving this point home over and over throughout this book, so listen up: you are a person of value.

In the societal marketplace, people are lonely and lacking leadership. In a world of scarcity, demand, and consumption, if you're a provider, a producer, and a wise leader who projects an example of goodness and good sense, people will pay you.

More importantly, they will pay you in loyalty, respect, and honor. You are exactly what the world needs you to be. You just have to be it.

CHAPTER 4

THE MOST ELITE
VERSION OF YOURSELF

*"When the present is painful enough,
you'll take the actions needed to change the future."*

This chapter is the last chapter of Part 1, which means it's a working chapter.

I am deliberate in the way I arranged this chapter. First, read it in its entirety. I will then walk you through a mental exercise, but you must read the whole chapter before participating. When you've finished reading every page of this chapter, close your eyes and go through the exercise.

Now I've got to warn you. This exercise will change your life because it changes the perception of who you are versus who you should be and can become. This is why I ask you to read through these pages first before participating.

Get used to me warning you throughout this book that if you're not ready to make a life-changing decision, you should stop reading and enjoy the information you've consumed. If you do decide complete this exercise, there's no going back.

Let me rephrase that. There *is* going back, of course, but you won't be able to unlearn what you've read. To go back is to live a life filled with excuses, a life unfilled, a life without.

Whether you make the decision or not to move forward on a new foot, you'll be clear on where you stand. You'll be clear as to whether it's even possible for you to be an example or not. So read this chapter carefully in its entirety and be sure to do the exercise.

BECOMING THE MOST ELITE VERSION OF YOURSELF

I call what you are about to do *The Most Elite Version of Yourself Exercise*. To get started, clear some space around you. Make sure you're in a safe place where you can stand up and close your eyes. With your eyes closed, turn your head to the right to look over your shoulder as if someone is standing next to you. Don't open your eyes until I tell you to. Keep them shut this entire time. With your head turned to the right, envision that the person standing next to you is the most elite version of yourself. That's right, this person standing next to you is the example, but it's *you*.

Imagine this most elite physical version of yourself as healthy, fit, energetic, and strong. Is that you now? Your midsection, legs, calves, thighs, chest, shoulders, and arms are sculpted and firm. Is that you now? As you go through this exercise, understand there's no wrong answer. The first answer that comes to your mind is the right answer. The second answer is your rationale, the excuse behind why you're not the most elite version of yourself right now.

Now back to your form. Zone in on the smallest details—your eyes, your brows, your ears, and your neck. For example, does the elite you have clear eyes, unblemished skin, and well-cared-for hands and feet? Is that true of you now? If not, that's okay. Remember, it truly is possible to be the most elite version of yourself.

Now, you've seen the most elite version of yourself naked. It's time to dress you up. If you were the most elite version of yourself, what would you be wearing? Your first answer is the right one.

Let's pivot our thinking a little bit now and talk about the elite inner version of you. If you're the most elite version of yourself physically, you must also be the most elite version of yourself emotionally. Think about who you are as the elite emotional version of yourself. What qualities do you have that attract people to you because they love being with you? Are you warm, trustworthy, funny, supportive, optimistic, reliable, and easy to be around? Consider qualities you admire in others that you want for yourself. Are these the qualities that you manifest now?

In this most elite version of yourself, people won't hang around you because they want or need something from you. They will be around you for one reason—*they just want to be with you.*

With your eyes still closed and your head turned to examine that most elite version of you, imagine how you feel. Meditate on your friendships, relationships, marriage, and family. Appreciate how you interact with everybody easily and how people admire, adore, and respect you.

Think of how you are performing financially. If you're the most elite version of yourself, you must be rich. You have your dream house, dream car, and dream spouse while raising your dream kids. Your imagined life is full of everything you want. White picket fences, pink poodles on the diving board, water beds for the hogs, air conditioning for the horses, Learjets on the runway, and SLs in the driveway, as an old song by the Earl Shaw Family of Eagles, goes. I wore that tape out.

The point is… you got it going on. Understand, all that materialistic stuff is just gravy.

The real gift happens when you transform into the greatest version of yourself and become the example.

Imagine how you would feel emotionally. You've got money. You've got love. You've got respect. You've got power. Yes, you've got it all. Take a moment and imagine what that feels like. With your eyes still closed, look at that person—you—and revel in who you can be.

Let's go further. Your eyes are still closed; your head still turned over your shoulder. Now, envision placing your feet into the footsteps of where the most elite version of yourself is standing.

Now, turn your head straight and open your eyes.

As you get accustomed to being back in your body, know this: that visualization exercise allowed God to show you who you can be. That's your potential in life. That's you as *the example*.

When I first went through this exercise, I did not look, act, talk, or feel like the person I am today. I had to become that person.

You might find it hard to believe, but I want you to know that visualization allows God to show you what's possible in your life. You can step into the greatest version of yourselves, and you'll do that one step at a time.

THE NEXT TASK

What I just walked you through and what I am about to talk to you about next is a lot to absorb. Focus on moving one step at a time into those elite feet.

The first step is having that vision. The second step is taking action to make that vision a reality. It won't happen overnight. But there is a process I call the *GCode* that will get you there.

The good news for you is that the book I wrote about the GCode (available on Amazon) comes free with the purchase of this book. I'm not out to make money from the book business. No, I am in the life-changing business.

The *GCode* is a life-changing book that takes you through a four-part daily process and leads you to become the most elite version of yourself. There are no gimmicks or upsells here. This is how it works.

THE GCODE

Gratitude

No matter what's going on in your life, you need a grateful mindset because gratitude is the precursor to abundance. If you are grateful for what you have now while in pursuit of what's next, that's the ultimate balance in life.

So before anything else, you must be grateful. What I am about to tell you next comprises a bit of wisdom, so write it down.

I know I've got to get grateful, so the first thing I do in the morning is write down five things I'm grateful for. That's what I want you to do, too. That's step one of the GCode. Do this, and you'll earn one point. Make it easy on yourself. Go to dailygcode.com, and sign up. It's free. You won't get any emails or follow-ups. How you perform is 100% on you.

Genetics

There's no way around it; being healthy is a mandatory part of the GCode. You need to work out and stick to a diet. In the app, you score half a point for each. Together, working out and eating right each day earns you one point. Combine that with the gratitude point, and now you've got two points.

Grind

Your grind is your job. If you go to work and hit your financial goal for the day, you get another point. If you want to make $1,000,000 a year, you better make $3,000 today. The trick is not to get overwhelmed and focus on the million. Just start thinking about $3,000 a day. Reach your grind goal, and you get another point.

Group

Group pertains to the group of people you spend your time with. Who did you invest your time in today? Did you go on a date night with your wife? My wife and I have been together for eight years, and we have a date night once a week. That's mandatory, no matter what.

I also have a date night with my kids, no excuses. With four children, I do a bit of juggling. I take the boys out riding and spend separate time with my daughter. This is my commitment: doing whatever I've got to do to ensure that I spend time with my family every week. It's non-negotiable. The same goes for my operators, employees, and friends. I go out of my way each week to make time for one of my friends and the people I work with. This is important because the group you hang out with dictates how you will spend your life.

My friend, Pastor Keith Craft of Elevate Life Church in Frisco, Texas, says your alignments (the people you surround yourself with) take precedence over your assignments in life. In other words, who you hang around dictates what you do in life.

That's why I believe the questions in the Group section about who you hang around with is the most important part of the GCode.

To recap: you need to address 1) Gratitude, 2) Genetics, 3) Grind, and 4) Group. You get one point each day per category. That's four points per day per month, which should give you a minimum of 100 points.

THE FORK IN THE ROAD

Now, you know who you have to be.

You know what's possible for you to be.

You know the daily steps, and I've given you a tracking mechanism for becoming that most elite version of yourself. There's nothing left but to do it.

At the beginning of this chapter, I warned you that you're at a pivotal standstill, a virtual fork in the road. Now, you must decide what you will do and who you will be.

Will you become the person standing next to you—the most elite version of yourself? If so, are you willing to do the work every day? Are you ready to do this even as you hit roadblocks—challenges and struggles—on the way to becoming the example? Or are you going to be a little bitch like everybody else? Make the decision. Because little bitches don't need to finish reading the rest of this book.

PART 2:
TRUST THE PROCESS

CHAPTER 5

THE BIG DECISION

"Life is a constant series of decisions.
Be sure you choose wisely."

Now you have a vision of what's possible and who you are capable of being in life, but you still have to make the big decision.

Do you really want to be that person you envisioned standing beside you?

I ask because—if you dive deep into your decisions—you've chosen not to be that person so far. You know what it takes to be an example—being fit, eating well, working hard, and being empathetic. If you are not the most elite version of yourself, that means you've made the decision repeatedly not to be that person.

That can change.

Make today, right now, the moment you decide to be that person. Do it because the world needs you.

I know this is a big decision. This is rededicating your life to become the best version of yourself. Remember, it doesn't matter what is in your past. It could be as bad or worse than mine. Make today the day you choose to become the best version of yourself.

Before you do that, ask yourself, are you willing to do what needs to be done to become that person?

If not, you should quit reading right now.

GETTING STARTED

I assume that you want to be a better version of yourself.

You want to strive for more.

You want more connections.

You want more powerful relationships.

You want more money or to buy back time and have less financial stress.

You want to be healthier and be a better version of yourself.

That's why you're here.

But *wanting* to be that person and
doing the work are two different paths.

The first step toward becoming that person is to want to become that person. That's the easy part. We all want to be the cool guy on TV. We all want to be the prom queen. We all want to be a hero. We all want to be a celebrity. But most of us never become the embodiment of our dreams because we're unwilling to do the work.

Today, we're going to change that. The rededication of your life isn't just wanting those ideals for yourself. It's committing to *doing the work* to *become* that example.

In the previous chapter, I defined the GCode and how you can rack up four points daily in the free app I designed. At the time of the writing of this book, my score on the app was 3,287. But my numbers are even higher than that because I've recorded my score for two years prior in Evernote, taking me to a consistent 1,000 points. That means in eight days, I'll hit 4,000 points. I've been on a 385-day consecutive streak without forgetting.

When I decided to become the example, I meant it. I'm willing to do the work every day. I'm out there doing what I promised myself I would do in the real world. I'm dedicated to what's required of me so I can earn the right to input data into my phone and earn that point. I don't take this lightly. The GCode is probably the most serious habit in my life. I am so serious about it that I got "GCode" tattooed on my neck, and I am not a neck tattoo type of person. I did it because I wanted that visual representation of my values ingrained where the world could see it, where everyone would know it was me. This is what it's taken for me to be the greatest version of myself.

THE DAY I ALMOST DIED (AGAIN)

In 2019, I broke my neck in a four-wheeler accident in South Texas. I had to be care flighted to a hospital. Doctors told me I was never going to walk again. That was a terrifying time for me.

But I had an edge, and it saved me.

I've been in the gym five days a week, every week, since I was 20 years old. At the time of the accident, I was 40. Due to those workouts, I could walk out of the hospital. I had prepared my body for the day it broke. I had put in the work every day for 20 years in the gym—with no excuses. I wasn't a big fat person who had lost a bunch of weight. I was a skinny person who had tried my hardest for 20 years to put on weight. No matter what I did to gain weight—the food I ate or supplements or hormones I took— I just couldn't do it. But in my mind, that didn't matter. I wasn't going to be deterred from my goals. I stayed at it, and it saved my life.

I didn't get any results for ten years, and I stayed at it.

I didn't get any results for 12 years, and I stayed at it.

Even when I thought, God, why haven't you made me the size of Steve Kuclo? I still returned to the gym.

On the day of my four-wheeler accident, I realized that it wasn't about me looking like Arnold Schwarzenegger or Steve Kuclo. It was about me being the best version of Ryan. The physical part of that meant going to the gym.

That crash broke my C6 and C7 vertebrae in my neck. The vertebrae didn't move out of place because my muscles were strong enough to hold them. If that had happened, it would've caused paralysis.

That said, I'm no doctor. And I know doctors read my books. So don't judge me for my medical lingo.

The point is I'm still here because I put in the work every day despite the results.

That's our motto in our office.

"We put in the work despite the results."

At that time, I'd put in the work to exercise for 20 years despite the results. When the moment came that I needed my muscles and strength to serve me, they were there. Had I skipped days, months, or weeks, I may not have been ready for that breaking point in my life. I might be writing this book to you from a wheelchair.

That's grit and what I want you to understand.

That level of commitment is what it takes to be that person—the person I envisioned standing to my right.

In the year 2000, I saw myself as a strung-out, skinny-as-fuck drug addict. I needed to get my life together, so I started working out.

I never stopped. It paid off 20 years later. I know it will pay off 20 years from now, too, because one of my standards is to take care of my health. I exercise to reduce my chances of having a heart attack or any other medical concern.

BUILDING FINANCES

When I made my first million dollars, I lost it all almost faster than I made it. But the takeaway was that I knew it was possible. Most people would've been devastated. My mindset was, "I got it once, so it should be easier to get it again." That's why I kept rising to the top despite what I faced. I was willing to do what it took to get the money I wanted. I did it legally, ethically, and with integrity... three more times.

My pledge to myself was that no matter what, I wouldn't take a regular job. No matter what, I wasn't going to be a regular person.

As an entrepreneur, I knew it was possible to become a millionaire again. All I needed was to be willing to do the work.

But this isn't about me. It's about you.

That's why you're reading this book—to become that example for yourself and others.

I'm already an example.

I don't make that statement to brag or be arrogant. It's factual. I've made the decision to be the best version of myself. I did the work it required. I'll continue to honor that decision and do the work.

WHERE ARE THE LEADERS?

The world around you is looking for a leader, and they need you to take the lead. They know you have it in you. What they don't know is how to motivate you to decide to better yourself.

Does this sound familiar? People might say, "Man, you got it going on." That's code for *they don't know how to tell you, but they can see you have greatness within you.* In my opinion, the word tracks you hear from people around you is God speaking through them to extract greatness from *you.*

Guess what?

When you step into becoming the most elite version of yourself, you lose weight. People start saying, "Wow, man, he lost weight. He looks really good. I wonder if I'd look that good if I lost weight, too?"

Step into that version of yourself, and you'll start inspiring people, but you won't even know it. When you start building your business, people might say, "She's really done well in her company. Maybe I should start my own." People might say, "He's a great father. I want to be a great father like him." "She's an excellent mother. I want to be an excellent mother like her when I have kids."

I'm sure you can see that being the example isn't just about you. It's about being the *best* you so you can extract the best of those *around* you.

As we discussed in the previous chapter, when you are the most elite version of yourself, the people in your life don't want handouts. They don't want money. They aren't trying to use you. No, they *love* you. They don't need anything from you because they are successful in their own right.

When you become that light in the world, other people turn into mosquitoes at night. They're attracted to your light. They want some of it. When you're the example, they'll think, *I want to be like them.* That's a big win for us. It's a big win for humankind because so many bad examples are out there taking up space. Having just one person at a time step up and show what is possible leads others to believe they *can* step up and be the example.

One of the biggest fights you will face that threatens being the greatest version of yourself comes from what I call the force of average. In the next chapter, we'll talk about fighting through that, so you can remain the most elite version of yourself.

All you need to remember right now is that there's a formula to follow to give you everything: commitment plus consistency equals success. It's that simple. Commit to a goal, stay consistent, and achieve success.

Let me give you an example.

THC PODCAST

In 2011, I started the *Hardcore Closer* podcast. It was called something else back then, but that's what it ultimately evolved into. My first episode had six listeners! I felt like a king. My second episode had zero. So did my third, fourth, fifth, and God knows how many subsequent episodes. In 2011, 2013, 2014, and 2015, I averaged 75-150 downloads an episode. Nobody was listening to my shit.

Most people would have given up. In 2018, when I was averaging 300-500 listens, I hung in there despite these dismal numbers. That's because I understand the formula of staying committed and consistent until I'm successful. It's not commitment equals success; it's not consistency equals success. It's...

Commitment plus consistency equals success.

In other words, I know I must stay committed and consistent until I see success. It's not even about expecting success. It's about staying put past the point of success.

I'm so glad I didn't bail.

In 2018, people started listening. In 2019, a million started listening. In 2020, during the pandemic, three million started listening. And now, the number grows daily.

I wanted to quit so many times.

Everybody else had a number one podcast.

My podcast has never been number one in the history of iTunes, but I stay consistent anyway.

That's just an example of what it takes—consistency with my podcast for the past 11 years.

As you now know, I've stayed consistent in the gym for 23 years. Consistency is the key to staying that person you dream about and want more than anything else to be. First, commitment, then consistency. Keep adding those up, and success is inevitable. I promise you right now that success is inevitable if you never quit.

You will become an example for others by doing the work and remaining consistent. And you will become an inspiration for everyone else watching —that, my friend, is the big payoff.

I wish it were smooth sailing from that point forward. But as I mentioned earlier, every time you stick your neck out, people are watching you. They see you winning. They know you're striving to be your greatest. Even as all eyeballs are on you, the force of average is after you. It's soulless, heartless, and doesn't give a fuck about you or your family. It's coming for you.

But you can beat it.

We'll talk about what it is and how you can do that in the next chapter.

CHAPTER 6

THE FORCE OF AVERAGE

*"We are at war, and the enemy is
more experienced than we are."*

In Chapter 2, I talked about how insane my life has been and how many mistakes I made along the way.

To reiterate: my family members were middle-class entrepreneurs who lost everything. I lost my father and gained an abusive stepfather.

This taught me that for every step up, there's a step down.

Newton's law applies to every action, meaning there's an equal and opposite reaction. I call that the force of average, or FOA.

DEFINING THE FOA

Imagine that this blue planet we're floating on is nothing more than a microchip. If you've never been inside a server room, let me describe it for you. Huge black cases with red and blue lights inside them line the walls. Who's to say our blue world is not just a light inside a giant server?

Track with me.

If you believe in God, please humor me, and read without judgment.

Picture that we're inside this blue planet—a microchip governed by rules, regulations, and laws. I'm not talking about mandates from the White House or the Kremlin. I'm talking about an algorithm that controls this planet.

I call it the force of average.

To put it in simpler terms, let's say that you're below average financially. You can qualify for social assistance programs, get on Social Security, apply for disability, and receive aid for your food and to support your children. All your needs could be met to give you an average life.

If you're an average person in America, specifically, you'll land in a decent tax bracket. You can shop at the normal stores and have a comfortable life. But the second you start chasing greatness to escape being average, the force of average gets angry. It tries to *push you back down* to average.

Conversely, if you're below average, the force of average will *lift you up*. It'll give you social assistance and all the money, food, and whatever else you need to live an average life. But the second you start striving for excellence and pushing past average, you mess up the grading curve for everybody else. According to its rules, you must get back in line.

Throughout your life, the force of average will attempt to push you down.

Think about it.

How many times have you had money and then lost it? The force of average got you.

You had love and then lost it. That's the force of average.

You nailed your dream job and then screwed it up. The force of average messed you up.

We all fall victim to it. Some of us daily, some of us monthly. It doesn't discriminate.

The force of average is designed to keep you comfortable. It is designed to keep you living an average life. In fact, everything on this planet is designed to keep you average.

Most people drive average cars. They live in average houses and are in average tax brackets with average jobs, average friends, average talents, and average discussions. This algorithm keeps society average, and the advantage to the people in charge is that it's easy to control those who are average. But it's hard to control greatness and excellence.

The biggest and only weapon the force of average has against us is very powerful—distraction. In America, specifically, we are distracted over 10,000 times a day by advertisements alone.[3] That means we see 10,000 different advertisements online, offline, on billboards, on cars, etc. On top of that, we have to make approximately 35,000 decisions per day.[4] That equates to roughly 45,000 points of fatigue and distraction. The force of average is, in itself, distracting.

Think back to when you tried your hardest and gained a little traction. You got laser-focused, in the zone, and accomplished your goal. But then the force of average swooped in and took all your trophies away. As soon as you lose your focus or step out of line, you lose everything, or at least any progress you've made.

How many people do you know who have worked their entire lives like robots? As soon as they reached their main goal, they sold their company, won the championship, made a bundle of money, and so on until they lost it all.

Evander Holyfield won a quarter of a billion dollars and spent almost all of it. Mike Tyson went bankrupt after winning $103 million when his

---

[3] https://lunio.ai/blog/strategy/how-many-ads-do-we-see-a-day/
[4] https://www.inc.com/heidi-zak/adults-make-more-than-35000-decisions-per-day-here-are-4-ways-to-prevent-mental-burnout.html

worth was four times that. Allen Iverson made massive amounts of money and ended up on the streets. I bet you could name someone personally who followed suit. That's the force of average at its finest.

If it can attack elite people, like athletes making millions of dollars, it's good enough to attack you and me. It uses that weapon of distraction to throw you off your goals and pull your attention to those 45,000 decisions and advertisements per day. It distracts you with gossiping people, and when you're striving for greatness, it takes the form of people saying things like, "Oh, you think you're better than us?" "You want to be somebody special?" And blah, blah, blah, on it goes.

SUPPORTERS OR REPORTERS

The people around you can either be supporters or reporters. Supporters push you up past average and guide you as they do so. Sometimes, they will even pull you toward excellence.

In contrast, reporters are the agents of average. They are the people who report to you and say things like, "You're too big for your britches." "She thinks her shit doesn't stink." They are the agents of average. They tell you, "I wouldn't do that." "That's a bad idea." "It's risky."

CONSPIRING MOFOS

The force of average and the agents of average conspire to attack you with distractions every day.

I don't know how many times people told me it was insane to try to build a business based on social media. But I knew they were just agents of average.

I also know we have a superpower within us as human beings. That superpower is under attack almost from birth. It is the ability to focus. I'm not referring to vision or eyesight, either.

In my world, vision plus action equals focus.

Focus is having a vision for what you want. It is knowing the end goal in your mind and taking action to make it a reality.

When was the last time you accomplished something super awesome—whether you finally solved that jigsaw puzzle or the multimillion-dollar problem in your business?

You were probably up all night, deeply ingrained in the problem. You were focused, in the zone, doing mathematic equations, crunching the numbers, pushing the shovel, whatever it took to get across the finish line; you were drilled in hard to make it happen. That's because you tapped into your focus superpower.

These are instances of powerful focus. But there is a flip side.

Ever since we were young, the force of average has been attacking our superpower. When we were kids, we might have heard our teachers or other adults say things like, "He can't pay attention." They might have tried to put us on ADHD drugs that weakened our attention and made us attention-dependent. If you ask me, ADHD should stand for *attention-dependent humans on drugs.*

The force of average is not done when we are young. It follows us when we become teenagers and adults. We might not know it, but we hear it. Have you ever said, "I'm a little scatterbrained," "I don't pay attention to details," or, "You know me... I have ADD."

Not only was the force of average formed as a weapon against us, but without self-awareness, we empower it. We're our own worst enemy.

When we're under the gun of the force of average, we need to practice focusing. But how do you turn it on to get in the flow and stay there?

We don't win by setting annual, monthly, or weekly goals. We win through daily wins. You can't turn off the force of average by talking about something you're *going* to do. You just *have* to do it.

Here's how I stay in the zone and focus: I depend on those four areas of my life that I take care of every day.

I need a grateful mindset.

I must take care of my genetics and make sure I'm in the gym. I must eat right.

I have to win in my grind and ensure I make money at my job.

Finally, I need to win with the group of people I surround myself with.

Every day, no matter what is tempting me, I stay focused and in the zone. I have to do these four things, despite how I feel or don't feel. Regardless of whether I want to do them, my feelings don't matter. I have to do them every day.

Knowing this, I turn off distractions. I don't put myself in a room with a TV on. I don't put myself in a room with the news playing. I don't put myself in a room with people who might talk to me as I focus on my four areas. Nothing will take me from what I have to do. One, I wake up and write down five things I'm grateful for. Two, I go to the gym. Three, I get ready and go to work. Four, I make sure to spend some time with my people.

With my group under control, I feed my head. Every day, I take my vitamins. I read books. I meditate. Completing all those tasks daily guarantees that I'm focused daily. Over time, I compound this interest. These wins keep me on task because I am committed to being the most elite version of myself.

You can do the same. I promise you, the most elite version of yourself is not a scatterbrained, ADD excuse-making motherfucker. I promise you, when God put your DNA strand together, that's not what he proclaimed your life to be.

Your job is to fight the force of average by staying focused and in the zone through the use of the GCode.

I reference the GCode repeatedly because it's the code to greatness and the foundation for your best life. Remember, great people are focused. The GCode will keep you focused and keep the force of average at bay.

Take it from me, just when you think you've won, and life couldn't be any better, the force of average will throw the fuck down on you like a UFC fighter. It will beat the living shit out of your amateur fighting ass. You've already been fighting for 20, 30, 40, 50, and maybe even 60 years of your life. The force of average has been around since the birth of this planet. It has been fucking up shit since the Big Bang.

You think you're going to win against it? No fucking way—unless you stay focused.

The only way I've discovered to win, whether I am talking about myself or others, is through the GCode and hitting those daily wins.

Dial those in, and you will be unstoppable.

Better, you'll fuck up the force of average.

CHAPTER 7

YOUR PERSONAL MISSION

"I'm here to help as many people as possible become the greatest version of themselves."

If you're going to stay focused, you'll need a mission.

In the previous chapter, we discussed the formula: vision plus action equals focus. Now, we need to distill that vision into your mission to take action.

Before we get ahead of ourselves, let me ask you: have you written down your personal mission?

I don't mean the shit you say in the back of your head or some fancy paraphrase you pull out of your ass when someone asks you. I mean, do you have a mission written down? My personal mission is "To help as many people as possible become the greatest version of themselves." That's my calling in life that I work at every fucking day.

In life, I am called to help as many people as I can become the greatest version of themselves. My focus on this mission led me to create the GCode, masterminds, books, and design seminars. I've connected people, built businesses, broken stigmas, created a solid track record, and kept all the receipts to prove it's possible.

I am not sharing this to run my score up or brag. I'm not that fucking guy. I have to share these details to prove what's possible, *so you will believe anything is possible.*

WELCOME TO CORPORATE

**Doing impossible shit is my calling.
But I didn't know that at first.**

2004 was my first full year as a banker and loan officer in Texas. It was also my first real corporate job. Back then, I thought I was making life-changing money—multiple six figures a year. I was convinced this was my calling. After all, I had read *Think and Grow Rich* and *How to Win Friends and Influence People.*

But I felt there was more to my dreams than being a loan officer. My calling was to house the homeless. That's what I did every workday. I thought *I am a loan officer, helping homeowners obtain wealth through homeownership. I am housing the homeless. I'm going to church and tithing. I'm buying rental properties. I'm helping investors make money. I'm helping real estate agents make money. I'm stimulating the economy around me like a rainmaker.* These were all the thoughts rolling through my head.

You can understand my logic with my family's roots in banking. It wasn't a big leap to think I was supposed to be a banker like my grandfather. But much like my grandmother, instead, I went to federal prison. Everything I had ever worked for was stripped from me.

At the time, I looked up at the sky and asked, why God? Why did you take this from me? I'm supposed to be a banker. Surely you don't want me to go back to washing cars. I'm supposed to be a banker. Why would you take this from me?

Looking back, I know my calling to be a banker wasn't real. I never felt fulfilled. It didn't matter that I made real money; I was empty. Fast-forward to the year 2010. The Dodd-Frank ruling shut down my ability to originate loans. As a felon, I could no longer hold a financial license.

This forced me to dig deep inside and discover who I was and what my true calling was. On the surface, I first thought it might be to help people with social media. Then I thought my calling was to help people make money. And then I thought my calling was to help people, period.

Now, I know my calling is to be a *greatness extractor*.

Once I stepped up and answered that call, I entered the best years of my life. Sure, it took a long time to hear the phone ring, but when I did, I became the example of what's possible in a world full of impossibilities.

That's one ending to the story. There's another ending—what happens to most people—and what happened to me, too.

In this scenario, we'll assume you're a banker making good money.

Besides being a little bitch, the force of average will complicate your life. Even though you're killing it as a banker, suddenly, you'll feel called to be a public speaker. You'll think, *why would I want to be a public speaker? I'm doing great as a banker.* That response is a distraction from the force of average. It's not a divine assignment from God. You need to be aware that this can happen and learn the difference between the voice of your calling and a distraction so you can get through it.

In 2005, I made $700,000 and read the book *The Law of Success* by Napoleon Hill.

After I finished the book, I jumped on the coffee table in my living room, like Tom Cruise on Oprah's couch. I looked dead in my girlfriend's eyes and said, "I don't know how I'm going to pull it off, but one day, I'm going to be a speaker. I'm going to change millions of lives. I'm going to teach people the things I've learned and applied to my life. This is my calling—what I'm supposed to do."

Then my stupid ass went to fucking work as a banker the next day. I did not heed my calling right away.

No matter that, God came into my life and said, "You've discovered it. You've got everything you could ever want in front of you, and the possibility starts right this second." Still, my dumb ass went right back to work the next Monday.

Why?

I decided to avoid the call because fuck, it's impossible. How am I going to do that?

A few months later, Monica Hubbard, my old broker, may her soul rest in peace, called me. She wanted me to attend special industry seminars and learn how to do mortgages, so I could start speaking at them. God was using Monica to push me where I was supposed to go. But I got it twisted and thought I was supposed to speak at the seminars to generate more banking business! *Yep, I'm supposed to become a human lead magnet.*

I didn't realize I had been handed a divine assignment. Life went on, and I avoided the call.

It wasn't until 2014 when I fully answered the phone and said, "Hello, what do you want?" It said, "We've been waiting for you."

Spoiler alert: the call was not about my car's extended warranty. No, this was a call about the rest of my life being the best of my life.

You can experience that same call seeking you out, too.

When you hear that voice in your head, it doesn't mean you're crazy. That's the voice of reason and possibility. It's showing you what's possible. The voice might also say to you, "Go be a speaker." In response, you might say, "But I'm making a lot of money as a banker." The voice may reply,

"You're going to change the world." And you'll shoot back, "I'm just trying to do my job." The voice will insist, "Go change your life and be an example." But you might still fight it: "I'm just trying to be comfortable."

Don't do that. Take action instead.

IDENTIFY YOUR MISSION

You need a mission because you won't follow your calling or listen to the voice if the change will only benefit you. Your mission must be bigger than you.

Notice that my mission isn't to get as rich as possible.

It isn't to make as much money as possible.

It isn't to be in as good of shape as possible.

My mission is about you.

It's about helping as many people as possible.

That's my mission today.

It's evolved from my first mission: to prove wrong every motherfucker who said I couldn't do anything right.

When I got out of federal prison the second time, my friends, family, and people around me all doubted me. They knew my *lucky streak* was over and that I was going to fail. They thought I would never have a comeback and make money again. Because I was a two-time failure, they expected the worst.

My mission at that time was simple: to prove to every motherfucker that I wasn't a motherfucker to mess with or doubt.

With that negativity hot on my heels, I passed up every doubter by hundreds of laps—if we were on the same track. I have since realized there's no reason for me to be mad at those people anymore. There's no reason for me to use negative emotions to fuel myself. That first mission was like racecar gas. It was good. It got me there fast and made my car angry. Learn from me. If you constantly burn it, you'll wear your engine down.

Try not to get to that point. Refuel with energy that won't be as stressful on your engine. A sustainable machine will take you down the road.

Your first mission might be to prove your haters wrong. Trust me, that's a good one. But at some point, you will reach your goal and prove them wrong. Then you have to move on to your next mission. That one must be bigger than you so you can help as many people as possible become the greatest versions of themselves.

It's okay to be fueled by rage and wanting to prove motherfuckers wrong in the beginning. But your mission needs to grow beyond that because you don't want to be an example of proving everybody wrong. You want to be an example of living what's possible. Resist being like the legions of people who earn F-U money or work at getting into shape only to stay miserable because they never refueled their mission.

Eventually, we have to refuel with abundance and a giver's mentality. We have to refuel with gratitude by following the GCode because that properly fueled mission keeps you focused.

Every time I wanted to quit my personal life mission, I was reminded by the voice in my head that I would lose my identity.

If I quit on my mission, I fail.

I refuse to fail.

If I failed, I would lose my identity as a winner because winners don't quit. My lifelong mission motivates and carries me for the rest of my life. It's simple but worthwhile.

It keeps me focused on the GCode and winning through my mission every fucking day of my life. I will continue to help people become the greatest version of themselves until I no longer have breath.

That's how big my mission is.

Remember, the world needs examples.

The world needs leaders.

The world needs us to be the people others look up to.

I'll strive to be that for the rest of my life no matter my circumstances, and I know I'll go out with a bang at the top of my game. Until I am dead, I will never give up and stop trying to be the best version of myself.

CHAPTER 8

YOUR PERSONAL VALUES

"If you are not clear on what it is you value,
then how will you know what the value is?"

As you're reading through this book, I'm assuming you're doing the work and that you now have a personal mission in life.

As a reminder, your mission is bigger than you.

It will drive you through tough times.

It will keep you motivated through the hard times.

It will teach you lessons through the struggle.

WHAT DO YOU DO WITH THAT MISSION?

You need values that support, govern, and matter to your mission.

Start by answering this question: what is it in life that you value?

When I speak to a room full of people and say, "Who in here has core values? Raise your hand." Everybody in the room will raise their hand. Of course, they will. Everybody perceivably has some personal or business core values that make up a part of their foundation.

Then I'll say, "How many of you have actually written them down?" About 70% of those hands will drop. Most people think *I hold my values inside my head. Because I value it, everybody else must value it as well.* That is incorrect; if others don't know what you value, how can you know if they hold the same values as you?

Next, I'll ask, "How many of you have them written down and say them out loud every day to the people on your team?" Zero hands will go up. That's because most people were taught to keep their values to themselves.

Sharing your core values with others is an important psychological breakthrough for you.

Here's something to ponder. Values, especially in America, typically correlate to money. This is the complication: people are usually told to keep their money a secret. That means most people keep their core values a secret.

Most people do this because their thought patterns follow: my family values may not be your family values. My religious values may not be your religious values. My ideology values may not be your ideology values, and so on.

Throughout our lives, we learn to keep our values to ourselves instead of being an abundant giver of value and sharing what we value. If we do this, we can align ourselves with other people who value similar things.

When we keep our values a secret, we wonder why we don't mesh with other people. We wonder why we don't fit in. We wonder why people are different from us.

This happens because we don't communicate what we value, and so we can't get to a mutual understanding of what we and others value. We won't know if we can value the same things and move forward together.

Instead, we keep our values discreet and secretive. This inability to communicate our values creates problems in all our relationships: work, play, family, and friends.

Not only do you have to figure out what you value, you also need to know who values it. Again, you'll have to share what you value. Make it what you stand for.

But what do you find valuable?

When people sit down to define their core values in life, they try to write some big, long speech. Remember, simple sells. In the Navy, they say, "Keep it simple, stupid." We like to say, "Keeping it simple sells here at Break Free Academy."

In Apex, simple sells ourselves. People not only share their values, but they do it in a way others understand. That makes relating to each other so much easier.

When talking to others about my core values, I state, "These are my four simple core values. Do you understand what I'm saying here?" I am trying to bridge that communication gap.

Of course, people understand when I break it down like that. I've made it easy for them to understand, communicate, and choose whether they value the same things I do. If they don't, it doesn't make them bad people. In that case, there are many things we won't be able to do together because we have a lack of congruency surrounding what we value. For instance, if we're doing business together, and you don't find money or hard work valuable, we can't go forward since money and hard work are some of my business values.

THE BIGGER QUESTION

Once you have defined your values, ask yourself, *am I a person of value?*

Back in the day, I thought my core values were honesty, integrity, hard work, love, and leadership. But I had to get real and ask myself, *am I living by those core values?*

We know the answer now. Old Ryan would say: hell no, I'm not living by these core values. I'm wound up like the E-string on the bottom of a guitar, boy. I am not living a life of tranquility. I am living a life of savagery on the warpath. Let's go. That's the way I love it.

Total disconnection.

Since I wasn't living those core values, I had to ask myself, why am I saying I value one thing, but my actions and life reflect that I value something else?

Inconsistency and incongruency surrounded what I said I valued. I assumed when outsiders looked at me, they knew what I valued. That was my ego talking, and it was wrong. I made decisions based on what I thought others' perceptions of me were.

If you're truly going to be a person of value, it isn't enough to define your values. You must live, breathe, and die by them—no matter who's watching. Values don't change.

You've heard me say this spin on an old quote before:

**"Methods are many, but principles are few.
Methods may vary, but principles never do."**

I live by it.

If I value integrity, I stay honest. I ask myself, *when was the last time I broke my word?* If the answer is never, I know I really do value integrity.

If I broke my word twice today, maybe I don't really value integrity. Maybe I need to work on the disconnect between saying integrity is a value and my actions not clearly reflecting that value.

Core values are nothing new.

Mission statements are nothing new.

But if we're going to be the example and the standard, we have to understand the values that make us valuable.

When I first went through this exact thought process, I figured *I don't need to share my core values. I've got them in my head.* That's a lie from the pit of hell. That's the devil manipulating you.

Second, I said wrongly, "I don't need to communicate them to other people." That's a lie, too. Do this, and you don't give other people a chance to understand your values.

When I decided what I valued and to become a person of value, living within what I defined as valuable—I made no excuses for taking the actions in my life to reflect that.

I was very exact: *this* is what I value.

If I'm going to be the example, I must become a person of value by *demonstrating* what I value.

That work takes place every day. I start with my daily mantras. These were written about six years ago from the time of the writing of this book. I wrote them myself because I needed an identity. So while they are daily mantras, in my notebook, I call them my identity statements. I still read these statements every single morning.

Someone gave me a picture of my personal identity statements that now hangs right next to my clothes above a shelf in my closet.

I see it every morning as I'm putting on my watches, and when I do, I read each of my 28 identity statements out loud. These aren't my core values. I'll give you those shortly.

I had to speak these statements into life to become what I was speaking. You have to say what you see so you can hear what you say.

When you speak your statements out loud and listen to your voice saying them, your mind prompts you to take action to create a new reality.

When I read these identity statements to myself every day, I become them.

MY IDENTITY STATEMENTS

Focus on my supporters, not the reporters. That means I don't give time to people who talk crap about others and engage in drama. I don't focus on those people. I focus on the people who support me, not those who report on me.

I only get mad when there's a purpose. As a naturally angry person, I stay honest about my tendencies and identify myself as someone who only gets mad—not *never* gets mad—when there's a true reason behind the situation.

I love myself first because if I don't, how can I love anybody else?

I think abundantly.

I show up in all four areas of my life, according to the GCode. I have a grateful mindset, and I'm mindful of my genetics, grind, and the group of people I spend time with.

My family of choice is greater than my family of origin. That means I choose my employees, business partners, kids, and wife. They are my family of choice and the people I choose to do life with. My family of origin is who brought me into this world. I did not choose them. However, I can make them my family of choice if I want to.

I honor everyone who's honorable, meaning I give honor to everyone who deserves it.

I listen intently. One part of my identity is that I *want* to be somebody who listens—that's how important this statement is to me.

I deserve everything I have. I did not cheat my way here, and I deserve it.

I'm focused on winning.

Be the example. This statement is why this whole book came about.

No distractions.

I think before I speak. As a kid, I was a blabbermouth and would blurt out anything. That's an identity that I don't want to have.

Be empathetic.

I live in the moment.

I pay attention to details.

Confidence is greater than cockiness.

Treat yourself.

Don't be an asshole.

I have patience for the less informed. This is directed at the people who argue online without having all the facts right.

If it's not done with integrity, I don't do it.

You can count on me.

I hold people accountable for their actions and words.

I make my own moves.

I identify my weaknesses and improve on them daily.

I'm focused on mastery.

My family gets the best. Everyone else gets the rest.

If I'm going to do it, I'm going to be the best at it.

I speak these 28 identity statements to myself every day because I am the example. I am the man I want to be.

When it comes to my core values, I keep them super simple. They must be easy to understand. Whether you are talking about personal or business core values, keep them short. I've chosen to be governed by my overall life core values, which connect to my goal of helping as many people as possible become the greatest version of themselves. These four core values support me in doing that.

MY FOUR CORE VALUES

1. I do what I say I'm going to do when I say I'm going to do it.

That's integrity. But the true definition of integrity can get a little muddy, so I'll simplify it. I want to be a person of value to you and live up to my word by showing you that when I tell you I will do something, I will do it.

2. I make no excuses.

This value is why I have a visible tattoo of "FYE" on my left hand. FYE stands for "Fuck Your Excuses." I can see it in any clothing other than a glove. Even though I wear nice watches, this tattoo stands out. And in this value, I'm not saying that to you as much as I'm saying it to myself. I don't allow any excuse to not go to the gym, not be successful, not be a good dad, be a failure, or be a bum. No excuses permitted. Period.

I don't make excuses. Does that mean I don't make mistakes? Of course, I make mistakes. The difference is that I own them. But I don't make excuses.

I make progress. I make wisdom. I make myself smarter through lessons learned.

3. I do the work.

If shit must be done, I will do it. Every day, I come into the office and work. I don't need to write another book. I'm doing the work to write one. I don't need to continue to post on Facebook, but it has to be done. I don't need to go to another meeting or speaking gig. Some of my investments pay more money than I ever dreamed possible. But I do the work anyway. Many people with my net worth aren't doing what I'm still doing. My work never stops.

4. I go above and beyond.

I'm a person of service. So if I'm a friend, I'm the best friend you could ever have. If I'm for you, I'm the best cheerleader. Period. If I'm on your team, I'm the best co-captain because I go above and beyond as a regular part of my life.

If I see trash on the streets, I pick it up. When I walk the trails near my house and spot garbage there, I throw it in the garbage. Why? Because I go above and beyond in *every* area of my life.

When I follow these four values, all the good bleeds over. I become a good father, a good husband, a good employer, a good leader, and a good friend —all because of these values.

In addition, I have found a good wife, good leadership in my companies, and good friendships. That's because the people around me value the same things. It's very clear to them what I value because I've been vocal about it from the beginning of our relationships.

Before you turn the page to the next chapter, I challenge you to write down your true core values. Communicate them. Get t-shirts and artwork made of them because they will guide you to be the example for the rest of your life.

CHAPTER 9

WHY <u>YOU</u> HAVE TO DO THE WORK

"We do the work."

It's time to design your life around your mission and core values. It's time to do the work. The easy part is thinking about it, writing it down, and even talking about it. But if we're going to be the example, we must do the work reflecting the example of our mission and values.

That's why at the end of the last chapter, it was critical that you took the time to create a mission and identify your core values.

With that accomplished, let's get to work.

When you went through the exercise of seeing the most elite version of yourself, the person you saw was most likely not who you are right now. Your values and mission are not what you've been focused on.

Not only that, but what you valued in the past is likely not what you'll value today. That's okay. At first, you decided to take steps to earn four points per day to become the greatest version of yourself. Now you're deciding to become a person on a mission. Your mission is to live according to your values.

At this moment, you must commit to doing the work to be the example for others to show them what works. There are no shortcuts. You don't get to be the example of not doing the work.

Part of being the example is doing what you are supposed to.

When people examine any success—whether it is losing weight, making money, having a loving relationship, successfully parenting, etc.—most see the result of the success in the now. It's easy for them to think the success was achieved overnight.

Everybody wants to get rich quick, lose weight fast, and only spend time on three-minute or six-minute apps—but not a second more. They want a pill to solve all their problems.

That's not how we do the work.

I don't want to be the example of a fucking shortcut.

I don't want to be the example of a cheater.

I don't want to be the example of a person who took a pill to change their life instead of doing the work.

You can call my philosophy hard-headed, stubborn, and maybe even ignorant. But as the example, I must do things the hard way to show others what's possible. How else can I preach that we (the people in my community) do the work? How can I preach that I go above and beyond if I'm not willing to do that?

Before we can work with the masses and get them to rise up to be examples in their own right, we must work on ourselves. We must be the example for them.

The first example starts with me; the second one is all you.

Your work needs to be done internally. Let's say you wrote down the core value of integrity, but you've been living a lie; that's okay. Now, you have a starting place.

I've been there.

When I first got on the internet in 2008, I was a loan officer dressed like Jake from State Farm. I'm talking khakis, a button-up polo shirt, the whole bit. Coincidentally, that happens to be what I'm wearing today—as I'm writing this book. But never mind that. Let's stay on track.

My point is that I didn't cuss, and I wasn't myself. I pretended to be this perfect person. You wouldn't recognize me today. I was like, "Hi there, I'm Ryan Stewman, the energy producer. And I'm so glad you're here..." *Who was that guy?*

It was a fake façade, but I thought I was being the example of what people wanted me to be. It wasn't until 2014 that I went on a podcast, and the host simply said, "So tell us your story." By then, I was so tired of hiding who I was and pretending to be a real-life hybrid version of Ned Flanders and Jake from State Farm. I was hiding two felonies, three divorces, and a miserable fucking existence. So, when I was prompted by that host, I just told the story. "I was adopted. I dropped out of school," and you know the rest.

More people connected with me after that podcast. They began paying attention to me. They started watching, listening, and catching my drift when I stopped pretending.

This was a massive turning point.

I understand that your life most likely isn't filled with divorces and felonies like mine is. So whatever secrets you're hiding, you need to fess up. Own that shit and become the example of what happens when you get over whatever it is you're using as an excuse to hold you back.

I want to be an example of a felon who turned his life around. I used to sell drugs. But I have come so far that I recently paid and bought a drug dog for a local police department with my own non-tax-deductible dollars.

I want to be the example of somebody who was adopted, who went on to change his life and built a name for himself with a name he wasn't originally given. I want to be the example of the dad I never had.

Now, it's your turn. Ask yourself, *what do you want to be an example of?* Tie the example you want to be to your mission and values.

I want to be the example of greatness and winning. Yes, that may sound arrogant to some people, but I'm winning because I'm putting in the work. I'm getting the at-bats. I don't consider myself great, but I'm on a quest for greatness, just like you. You should strive for it, too. That's much better than not caring and being the example of average and failure.

When I thought about my life and considered my path, I had choices in front of me. As you know, it's not like me to take the easy road. I didn't approach my next steps with an average mindset. I didn't want to get just any job. I shot higher.

I wanted to be a felon who turned his life around and became a billionaire. I wanted to be a felon who turned his life around and became a world leader. I want to be a felon who turned his life around and changed the face of certain industries.

I'll get there because I'm willing to do that work.

I'm willing to show up to the office every day before anybody else.

I'm willing to stay later.

I'm willing to pick up the trash. I'm willing to wipe down the sink.

I'm willing to clean the toilets, mop the floors, and do whatever it takes.

I'll do it, and I've proven that.

Being the example is what's created the culture around us. It's what has attracted people like you to read this book.

When you become a better person, you become the example of someone who's done the work on themselves. When you've done the work and become financially free, you become the example of someone who's earned their money. It wasn't given to you. You earned it, and that is a crucial difference.

When you do the work in your relationship, you become the example of someone who's built an amazing connection with their spouse. It doesn't matter what area of life we're talking about; success and winning all come from doing the work.

If you're going to have an amazing relationship, for example, you have to give up your right to be right. It's hard. But you can't let that be an excuse to stop you.

If you're going to make a whole bunch of money, you need to give up some of your time. Yes, it'll be hard, so what? Keep going.

If you're going to be in great shape, you have to go sweat in the gym to get there. It's going to be hard—do it anyway.

As the saying by Ashy Bines goes, "You get to choose your hard." You can choose to have a hard life full of sickness, miserable relationships, and emptiness. That's hard. Or you can have a hard life full of sweat in the gym, working on yourself, and giving up your right to be right so you'll have better relationships. You get to choose that hard.

You actually do the work and become the example through the hard ride. And the harder you work, the easier the hard work becomes. That's a fact.

I see people coming into the gym to work with my trainer. He can put them through the wringer. In the first session, he asks them to do burpees and squats. If the person is slightly overweight, it kills them. They're sweating to death, breathing hard, bent over, dying, splashing water all over their face.

The next day they come in, and it's the same thing.

A week later, the same thing.

Two weeks later, they're not breathing as hard.

A month later, they're not breathing hard at all.

Two months later, they're moving a little faster even though they're working harder.

Remember this when you need it: when you work hard, hard work becomes easy. Most people never find that out. They work hard for a short time and think it's not getting easier, so they quit.

Here's what they don't know. If you quit working out on week one because it's hard, you'll never realize how easy it will be on week six, week 12, or week 900—which is closer to where I'm at.

Stick to it, and you'll become an example of consistency. Consistency is a power move.

As you and I both know, the world's got a serious lack of consistency, so there's a lot of value in becoming an example in that area.

CHAPTER 10

THE WORLD NEEDS YOU

"There's a strong demand and a
lack of inventory when it comes to examples."

Right now, there's no example of what you are capable of anywhere in existence.

No one can do what you can do.

No one's capable of achieving what you can achieve.

No one's capable of the greatness in you that only you possess. That's your unique gift.

Three billion genome base pairs make human beings about 99.9% similar to other humans around us.[5] Within a species, including humans, typically there is a 0.1% or (1 in 1,000 difference of the "letters" that make up a DNA sequence).[6]

Because there is only one you, there are no examples of what that 1 in 1,000 in you is capable of being. That solely belongs to you. That means the world needs you to find, define, and mine your .1%—the part that no one else is capable of doing but you.

That difference in percentage—your signature DNA—is still vulnerable to the force of average. It sneaks into people's minds and fucks them up, derailing them from their calling.

---

[5] https://irp.nih.gov/blog/post/2018/11/three-billion-base-pairs-vs-one-powerful-computer
[6] https://scientificinquirer.com/2018/06/07/humans-are-about-as-genetically-diverse-as-any-other-animal/

You have a unique assignment on this planet, all based on that difference in your DNA that is yours alone. It is unique from anybody else's assignment on this planet. You have to protect it because the force of average will sneak in and tell you that the defining percentage of you is stupid. It'll whisper that you're different and that nobody else will be the real you. It'll lie to you and say that nobody else cares about it and that it's just a stupid human trick. It will do its best to convince you that it's a curse, not a blessing and that what makes you special is not to your advantage. The real truth is that this is your advantage. It's a threat to the force of average that knows that when you tap into your mission and values along with your unique DNA, you can become the true example we all need. That's why you are battle-tested.

Your special difference takes you from a soldier strolling the streets to becoming a fucking tank patrolling them. The best part is that as you lead the way, refine who you are, and rewire your mind to become a better person, the more you're transformed into an example.

I always tell people that being in sales is a personal development plan with a pay plan attached to it. The more you become personally developed, the more money you will make. The more you become personally developed, the more connections you will make.

The more you become personally developed, the more people you will inspire, and the more you will become the example.

Here's the sad fact: great examples are rare. At the beginning of this book, I asked you to identify some examples of people who have lived a great life.

When I ask people that question, most can't give me more than two names.

Since examples are an endangered species, this is your opportunity to be one. You've got the blueprint. You've got the framework. You can see the elite version of yourself, identify your mission and values, and do the work.

My mentor, Pastor Keith Craft, once told me, "When I go out to eat at a Mexican restaurant—my favorite food—I can't have a margarita. I can't have a glass of wine. I've never drank an alcoholic beverage or had a sip of alcohol in my entire life. That's not because I'm a preacher. It's because I'm the example."

He went on: "If a gentleman walks into my church struggling with alcoholism and I help lead him to the Lord, who steps in his life and breaks that alcoholism, if he sees me, the preacher, at the local Mexican food restaurant drinking a margarita, I might change his mind. He might reason; *if the pastor can do it, I can, too. That makes it okay.* He might go back to alcohol. I have to be the example of a guy who has chosen a life without it."

I'm not a pastor, so I do occasionally drink, but I don't do drugs. I tell people all the time that drugs are bad.

This follows because my example is integrity.

I don't break my word.

I don't cheat on my wife.

I don't steal from people.

I don't show up with my hand out.

I'm a giver.

I want to be the example of those values, so I choose to always take the high road.

God blessed me with my uniqueness so I could be a gift to the world unlike anyone else's. And God blessed you with your difference so you can do the same thing. But if you don't define and refine your unique gift, you'll never be able to give it to the world. You'll never be seen as valuable because you're not giving something to the world that is worthy of receiving value.

The world needs you to step up and live by the values you've written down.

The world needs you to step up and follow your mission.

The world needs an example to look up to.

We live in such a vacuum of greatness; it's unreal. But I know this. You're on this planet with a unique mission. With your signature DNA and your willingness to focus on your mission and act, you can be 100% certain you'll succeed.

Once you've decided on your direction, beware! The force of average will try to convince you that you're too weak, not rich enough, not strong enough, not good-looking enough, not big enough, not small enough, not fast enough, not slow enough, too tied down, too busy, and so on. The force of average will try to convince you that you are all these negative factors.

What you really are is vastly different. You are designed with your uniqueness to do what no other man or woman on this planet can do. When you tap into that and go on despite the odds, setbacks, friction, restrictions, and anything else designed to throw you off your game, the world will know it. They'll see it because they've been looking for it. They've been looking for you. They know they need the example.

When you become the example, the world knows it because it lacks examples. We look for them every day.

Take this as a sign that people need you to show them what is possible in today's chaotic existence.

Even if you're reading this book hundreds of years in the future, the world still needs examples. There will never be an abundance of examples of greatness. There will always be an abundance of examples of failure and being average.

Greatness is a scarcity.

Great people are an endangered species.

Striving for greatness is worth every bit of the work and effort. I hope you use the unique gift you've been brought here to share.

CHAPTER 11

BECOME THE EXAMPLE

"Be the person you would look up to."

Your next step is to become the example. The purpose of this book is to provide you with the necessary steps to elevate you to the top of your game. It is to help you become the most elite version of yourself so that you can be an example for those around you at all times.

To become the example is your responsibility. Ignoring it will not make it go away. If you decide to go forward with a road map of your mission and values, you *have to* become that person—*one step at a time and one day at a time.* It's not one year at a time, one month at a time, or even a week at a time. You literally will take one day at a time. When you are the example, you need to represent what winning looks like at every moment of every day.

WHAT WINNING IS NOT

Before we talk about what winning looks like, let's get honest about what winning is not.

Winning's not being drunk or partying at the club all the time.

Is it okay to get drunk occasionally?

Is it okay to party in the club now and then?

Maybe, but don't fool yourself...

**Winning is winning in your relationships.
It's winning in your business. It's having a winning mindset.
Winning is having a good healthy body.**

As a parent, my job is to demonstrate balance at home and at work. It's my job to be a good father to my kids, a loving husband to my wife, an influential leader to my employees, a supportive mentor to my clients, and an upstanding member of my community. That's how I can be the best example.

I don't want to be the wrong example by partying late at night. I'm not shitting on you if you like to party. I'm just saying that's not in the cards for me. Being called to be the example means not doing those things.

Here's another thing that winning is not. Winning is not bitching, arguing, complaining, and moaning, whether it's about politics, your situation, or gossiping about other people. Winners don't get wrapped up in people's drama. Nothing's worse than people on social media who are constantly bitching about the president.

Winners talk about what they've done and what they're going to do. Sure, it's okay to share a political meme occasionally, but don't make it a habit.

Winners stay inside our area of influence and remain focused. We're an example of winning inside and out. Winners live by the GCode, the code to greatness, four points at a time.

When you get dialed into the four areas of the GCode: gratitude, genetics, grind, and group—you become the example of what it looks like to be the greatest version of yourself. Do this, and you will find that you are a magnet.

You will draw people to you.

You will attract people to you.

People will want to be around you.

They'll feel your vibrations and want to download your wisdom.

They will want some of your winning qualities to rub off on them. Being the example is a very attractive human quality.

When you represent what winning looks like at all times and are living by the GCode to become the greatest version of yourself, you morph into a person people admire.

Each day I strive to be the example of somebody I would respect. I've said this several times throughout this book, but it's a point I want you to remember, so I will say it again. If I can give people something to respect and believe in, I am the example.

The same is true of you. If you can give people something to respect and someone to believe in, you'll be the example for them. It all starts with being the person *you* would admire.

Would you look up to someone who's drunk all the time? No.

Would you look up to someone who cheats on their spouse? No.

Would you look up to someone in financial ruins? No.

Would you look up to someone who's extremely out of shape and unattractive and who chooses not to do anything about it? No.

I'm being real with you. You can get mad at me for the words written in this book, or you can take to heart what I am saying. You need to understand that if you're going to become the example, you have to be the example across the board.

So few people are willing to do that. That scarcity is your advantage. When you become a person people look up to, they'll start putting you on vision boards on their computers, phones, and in their houses. People have pictures of me with my jet and cars because they want that to be their life. I've set an example of what's possible for them.

Given where I've come from, it's the greatest feeling in the world. I'm a two-time felon and three-time divorcee who was adopted, abused, and on the wrong side of life. If I can be the example, and be on people's vision boards, what's your excuse?

You have such a competitive edge and advantage over me in every way possible. There's no reason that you can't lead and become a better example than I could ever be. You don't have my baggage. You don't have my failed stories. You don't have my days in prison. But you do have the chances, opportunities, and abilities to become the example, to be who people honor.

Follow this path, and you will become the person that you would honor. That's how you become the example for yourself. That's when other people see you as an example for them. Then people start to gravitate toward you. They want to partner with you. They want to spend their time with you. They want to enhance your experience on this planet with them. They want to show you ways to make more money, get in better shape, take better care of your health, have better relationships, and stimulate your mind more. All because overall, you improved as a human being.

People need you to stay the example, and they're willing to help you maintain your exemplar status.

Remember, you owe your uniqueness and greatness to the world—that's how you become the example. You owe it to yourself. You owe it to your present or future kids to be the example. I want you to become the example.

If your dad never told you anything positive or encouraging, let me be the voice of Father Ryan right now. Please know that I believe in you. You've already proven you're serious because you've read so much of this book.

Remember, you've made it this far because this is important to you. It's also important to the world. People need you. Don't forget that you have it in you to do this. Whatever excuses or reasons, no matter how real and logical they seem, for not becoming the example are from the force of average. Recognize that it's trying to keep you from showing the world what's possible through hard work, integrity, ingenuity, and grit. You, my friend, are that person—the example we all need.

It's time for you to take action. I'll see you in the next section.

PART 3: CONSISTENCY OF CHARACTER

CHAPTER 12

THE DISCIPLINE

"Everyone wants to be rich.
No one wants to do this hard-ass work."

Wikipedia defines *discipline* as "action or inaction that is regulated to be in accordance with a particular system of governance."[7]

As a child, if we got into trouble, we were disciplined at home or school. Due to our exposure to discipline as kids, when we become adults, we find the word *discipline* synonymous with *punishment*—so we run from it. In truth, discipline is a form of self-governance that guides us and keeps us consistent. If you refuse to re-examine the meaning behind the word *discipline,* you'll never reap its benefits. The force of average is applauding your refusal—that's just one of its many tricks. Don't listen to that liar. It truly takes discipline to become successful. It takes discipline to build character. It takes discipline to be a leader. It takes discipline to be in good shape and healthy.

People who don't have discipline live off Butterfingers and chocolate milk —just like little kids want to do. In contrast, people who have discipline eat vegetables and proteins and drink water. They follow a disciplined regimen that keeps them in shape and healthy.

Discipline is not punishment. Discipline is self-control.

---

[7] https://en.wikipedia.org/wiki/Outline_of_thought

THE MECHANICS OF SELF-CONTROL

Maybe you've noticed that anytime you've tried to have self-control and be disciplined against the temptations on this planet (which are everywhere), the force of average uses its number one weapon—distractions—against you.

In this scenario, the word *distraction* is synonymous with *temptation*, and it is everywhere. That's why you must have discipline. You have to master the ability to take action or inaction, depending on which is needed, to resist the temptations and distractions from the force of average.

For example, you need discipline to show up for your health every day by exercising and sticking to a diet. Not some days. Not five days a week, and not six days a week. You have to show up for yourself *every fucking day.* You can't do that without discipline.

As I shared with you earlier, I've had the discipline to go to the gym five days a week, every week, for the last 23 years. I don't like it. I've never liked it. I do like the results I get from going to the gym. Sometimes I enjoy the feeling I have after I go to the gym. But I don't dig going there or exercising. I'm not one of those people. It's pleasurable for some people but not pleasurable for me.

What enables me to keep winning in this area is that I have the discipline to work out every single day—no matter what. If I don't physically go to the gym on a rare day, I'm actively walking the trail by my house or doing labor around my home. I don't have a day off. I have governed myself to exercise daily.

My friends Andy Frisella and David Goggins call the voice that whispers "go back to sleep" the inner bitch voice.

Every day when I wake up, that inner bitch voice is the first voice to talk to me. I'd like to say that I wake up, hear God's voice, and it gets me motivated. I want it to sound like Bishop T.D. Jakes, or something like that, and get me all pumped up, but that's not the case at all.

Instead, this inner bitch voice shows up and plagues me. Hey, you ain't gotta get up and get on the GCode. You ain't gotta go to the gym, man. You deserve to sleep. You earned it. You got money in your bank account. You got a full stomach. This voice argues with me to take the day off every fucking day.

It's my job to face off against that voice. I treat it as if it's a hater on the internet telling me I'll never be shit. This is a sample of the role-playing I hear in my head:

Inner bitch: Yeah, I'm not going to get up and go to the gym.

Me: You must have me confused with somebody who's a bitch, little inner bitch voice. I'm telling you, I'm getting up and going to the gym.

On my way to the kitchen, the inner bitch voice nags at me, "Hey, you can still go back to sleep. You're half asleep anyway."

I don't pay it any mind and get on with my routine. As soon as I hit the kitchen, I go to the refrigerator and crack open an energy drink. Taking that first sip silences that inner bitch voice.

I let it know I'm not taking a day off because I'm taking in energy to take the day on—not take the day off. Of course, it would be exciting for me to spend my money on an exotic vacation somewhere or take time off and blow cash on stuff I would love to do. But I understand that boring builds big. One of my mentors, Bobby Castro, who wrote the foreword of this book, just exited his business for over a billion dollars. "Boring builds big" is one of the lessons he taught me. Bobby got where he's at by not doing the glamorous CEO shit you see on TV. He's done the mundane stuff day in and day out. That takes discipline.

That's me. I'm boring. Day in and day out, I'm writing books. Day in and day out. I'm making Facebook posts. Day in and day out, I'm speaking on the stage. Day in and day out, I'm in sales meetings with employees. Day in and day out, I either attend or lead company meetings with controllers. Day in and day out, I'm in finance meetings with boards of investors and companies where I sit on the board. Day in and day out, I'm doing the unglamorous stuff to move this needle. I'm sitting through meetings with lawyers and meetings upon meetings about meetings that we're going to have meetings about. All that number-crunching and paperwork has to be done—even though nobody else wants to do it.

My ability to stand firm and do all this boring stuff is part of my uniqueness. It allows me to do the boring work and build something big.

That same quality correlates to the discipline to take care of my body, go to the gym, and do the same boring reps. What sucks and is boring every day builds big. That's how bodybuilders get jacked. They go in there and execute the same boring bench press each week. They complete the same boring squats day after day. They know that boring builds big, too.

Most people won't do these boring tasks because they have an incessant and insatiable need to be entertained.

Boring gets you ahead. When you have the discipline to do the boring work, despite the lack of instant results and whether you want to or not, it puts you light years ahead of everyone else. You get the advantage because everyone else is scared to death to be bored.

When you are willing to embrace boredom, the mundane, and most importantly, discipline—not as a form of punishment, but as a form of advancing your character—you will beat everybody else at the game.

If we're going to build your character to be the example, you need to be an example of consistency. Consistency is missing from many people's lives. Nail down this aspect of discipline, and you will show people that you are the example—because you are fulfilling it.

Another one of my sayings is: "I'm not going to start anything that I'll stop." I rarely quit anything. Months ago, I had a hair transplant, and I still take the pills I was prescribed for it. My nails and everything else the pill targets are growing. I committed to taking these vitamins because the doctor told me they are natural supplements that support my health. That's all I needed to keep going. I'm all in.

Ten years ago, I committed to writing 5,000 words every day on the computer. I still do that to this day. Because of my consistency, I am one of the greatest writers in the game right now.

Consistency is what's developed me into the man I am today. Through my constant actions, I have learned:

If you do what others won't, you'll have what others don't.

Many people won't do shit. They won't be consistent. They won't develop discipline. They won't put in the work or time. They chase shiny objects. They'll leave whatever they're concentrating on and promise to follow through on their next endeavor. That's never going to work, and they're never going to get anywhere.

If you have the discipline to stay plugged in and keep your head down, you will win. You will become the example.

The best part is you will also improve. It's great to have outsiders look up to you and notice that you have discipline, character, and consistency, but that's nothing compared to becoming a better you.

It all begins with having the discipline to say no to that inner bitch voice and do the boring work even if something exciting is tempting you. I've been invited to some of the coolest shit ever plenty of times, but I had work to do and couldn't go.

In retrospect, all I can say is, thank God I didn't do the fun shit. The boring shit is what's paying my bills these days.

CHAPTER 13

INTEREST PAID ON INTEGRITY

"Your word is either worth gold, or it's worthless.
There's no in-between."

One of the biggest forms of currency is integrity. You can always borrow money if you're a person of your word. Somebody will loan it to you. You can always be trusted with anything because someone will trust you. As long as you keep your word and remain a person of your word, integrity pays interest.

My favorite story in the Bible isn't religious. It's from the book of Genesis about a young man named Joseph:

"Now Israel (Jacob) loved Joseph more than any of his other sons because he had been born to him in his old age (Jacob had several wives. His favorite was Rachel, Joseph's mother), and he made an ornate robe for him. When his brothers saw that their father loved him more than any of them, they hated him and could not speak a kind word to him." (Genesis 37:3-4).[8]

A coat of many colors at that time signified royalty. In my head, I imagine Joseph receiving the coat and strutting around, saying something like, "I'm dad's favorite, and I'm special," as he danced around the room.[9]

The next day, Joseph and all his brothers went out to work. The brothers had conspired to harm Joseph and abandon him in a field. They initially

---

[8] https://www.christianity.com/bible/niv/genesis/37-3-4
[9] https://www.christianity.com/wiki/bible/story-of-josephs-coat-of-many-colors-and-its-meaning-today.html

threw Joseph into a hole, allegedly shredded the coat, dipped it in animal blood, and were going to leave him to die.

They planned to show the coat to Jacob as proof that Joseph had been killed by a wild animal. But they retrieved Joseph from the hole when they met up with a slave trader. They sold their very own flesh and blood to that man. The slave trader sold Joseph to a man in Egypt named Potiphar, the captain of the Pharaoh's guard. When the brothers arrived home, they told their father that Joseph had died, and Jacob was heartbroken.

Meanwhile, Joseph went to work for Potiphar as a slave, and due to his integrity, became his second in command. He outworked everybody and soon was the most powerful person in Potiphar's household.

One night, Joseph was alone, working in the kitchen. Potiphar's wife came in and dropped her robe; she was butt-ass naked. She looked at Joseph and said, "Do you want to get some of this?" (I'm obviously paraphrasing here.) But remember, he was a man of integrity, so he said, "No, I refuse to do that behind Potiphar's back." This embarrassed the wife. She ran out of the room and told people Joseph had raped her. Joseph got thrown in jail.

While in jail, Joseph met a cupbearer (wine pourer) and a baker. They were locked up because they had offended their ruler and master by misinterpreting the Pharaoh's dream. When the cupbearer and the baker told Joseph about the Pharaoh's dream, Joseph said, "Tell the Pharaoh I know what his dream means. I'll be more than happy to share it with him if he'll simply get me out of jail." So, the cupbearer and the baker, eager to make the Pharaoh happy, told the guards, who then took Joseph before the Pharaoh.

Joseph told the Pharaoh that the dream meant there would be seven years of harvest followed by seven years of famine. He advised that they store what they harvested to get through the famine. Basically, Joseph gave the Pharaoh a 14-year economic plan.

Sure enough, they harvested and stored everything for seven years. In the eighth year, the drought came as Joseph predicted. As the drought endured, people from other cities and countries came to plead for some of the stored harvests.

Because of his economic plan for the Pharaoh of Egypt, Joseph became number two in charge. In the twelfth year of the drought, Joseph was asked to meet with a group of people from another country. As he looked around the room, he realized the meeting was with his father and brothers, who had come as representatives of their hometown. They planned to ask for some of the surpluses the Egyptians had wisely stored in their tombs. After 12 years, Joseph's father had thought him dead, and his brothers thought he was a slave, so they did not recognize him at first.

After his father and brothers pled for the food and supplies, Joseph said he would give them what they needed. Then he said, "Here's what I want you to know and why I'm giving you all this. I am your son Joseph. And while you did things to me that you meant for evil, God meant it for good."

Joseph's story is one of the most powerful stories in the Bible. Because what puts us in a position of struggle—as was the case with Joseph when he was accused of rape—ultimately leads us to where we are supposed to be. If Joseph hadn't been accused of rape, he wouldn't have gone to jail. If he hadn't gone to jail, he wouldn't have been able to interpret the Pharaoh's dream. If he hadn't been able to interpret the dream, he wouldn't have been able to come up with his economic plan. And if he hadn't come up with the economic plan, he wouldn't have become number two in the country.

Often, when you're being tested, what God or the Universe are testing—depending on what you believe—is your integrity.

Joseph could have fucked that chick, but he didn't.

Joseph could have cut corners, but he didn't. He chose to have integrity.

Joseph could have told the Pharaoh he had to pay him money to get the lesson, but he did the right thing.

Since my personal story and background are crazy, Joseph's story resonates with me. That's why I like it so much.

In 1999 and 2000, when I got busted for selling drugs, I had every opportunity to snitch on the people around me. I knew their names, addresses, how much money they had, and how much dope they had moved. I knew it all. But even as a drug dealer, I had integrity and didn't snitch on anybody. Pull my papers. It's all good. I have the receipts to prove it. I didn't snitch on anybody, not a single soul.

Instead, I did my time. I could have walked away completely free if I had snitched. As a young white kid with a bright future, I could have gotten off just by telling on a few minority outcast members of society. But I chose integrity and no one got in trouble but me. I needed to do my time since I did the crime.

Five years later, when I was wrongly accused of a crime that I didn't commit, I plea-bargained down the charge. That's when I did 15 months in federal prison. The guys I did not snitch on in 2000 were in there with me. They had gotten busted on their own.

Had I snitched on those guys and been in the same prison with them, they would've killed me.

Instead, they introduced me to this dude named Wawa. Because of that, I started teaching the other inmates how to clean up their money when they got out so they could start a new life. I changed lives while I was in there. My integrity allowed me to do that. It was easy for people to trust me because they saw how I operated. My integrity allowed me to become a person of influence—even in a place where people aren't very influential.

My integrity paid off. The point of my story is not about going to prison or snitching on people. The point is to keep your integrity. If you did the crime, you do the time. If you made the mistake, you cover the bill.

My friend, John Cheplak, shared a quote from one of our Million Dollar Mastermind stages. He asked the audience, "If you are parked at a red light and get rear-ended, whose fault is it?" The first, second, and even third answers we heard were, "The person who rear-ended you." John looked the audience right in the eyes and said, "No, it's your fault because you were at the red light in the first place. That's where you were supposed to be."

When I went to prison the second time, I asked God, "Why am I in here, God, when I was doing everything right? Why do you have to put me in this position? Why do you have to burn me like this? Why did you do me this way?" Poor Ryan, the victim.

I now realize all these years later that I wouldn't have that story for you. I wouldn't have learned those lessons. I wouldn't have made those connections. I wouldn't have gathered that street cred to be where I am right now.

As many times as I wanted to cheat, lie, steal, or snitch to get ahead or out of trouble, I made a power move and kept my integrity. Holding steadfast to it is the only reason I'm here.

If you are not living with integrity, it's never too late to change. Remember, integrity pays *big* interest.

Here's an example. The other day, a very wealthy friend of mine called me. I'm not going to divulge his name in this book, but he said, "Stewman, you know what? I've known you for five or six years now, and you never ask me for shit. You never want shit. You never ask me to invest in your shit. You never want to borrow stuff. You're the only friend I have who has never asked me for anything. I'm going to send you a million dollars in crypto. What is your wallet address?"

Many people show up to relationships without integrity and intention. They think I'll be friends with this person because they're rich. Once they like me, I'll get them to invest in my fund or startup, do my real estate deal, or whatever. I just show up with intention and integrity without any expectations.

Sometimes how I show up goes unnoticed or ignored. But that doesn't change who I am. Let me repeat. *I do the boring work.* Living my life with integrity is boring. Choosing not to go to the club with all the hot chicks late at night when I'm on the road is the epitome of integrity. I'm in my hotel room by 10 o'clock. Why? I don't want to get in trouble being out late at night: I'm committed to integrity in my marriage. It's not easy, but it's worth every bit of it.

The story of my friend giving me a million bucks is just one of many. A million bucks may or may not impress you and may seem foolish, but my friend had it to give. The takeaway is that I would have never gotten this far if it hadn't been for integrity.

Don't forget, integrity isn't a dollar amount. It's a disciplined amount.

CHAPTER 14

REAL INFLUENCE

"Live your life like everyone is watching you on a live cam."

In 2020, when the world was going through panic and a pandemic, I decided to adopt my son, Asher Stewman.

Asher is Amy's son from a previous relationship. His father is not very active in his life. If something happens to his mother, I would hate for Asher to go back to his father and have his quality of life and lifestyle changed. I would hate for him to miss out on his brothers, with whom he's grown up since he was two years old.

I proposed to Asher's father that I adopt Asher and assured him he would have access to Asher. I just wanted Asher to have my name and be his legal guardian if something happened to my wife, Amy. Maybe you're thinking, *that sounds easy. The dad's on board. You just need to sign a few forms, and you're done!* Not when you're a two-time felon with three divorces. The courts tend to frown on that. We had to Zoom with the court for the adoption because everyone was meeting digitally.

Still, we pushed through. The whole ordeal cost me about $15,000. When I adopted Asher, it was a big day—July 19th, 2021. The very next day, his sister, Harlyn, was born. I got two more kids in two days!

After it was all said and done, I said to Asher, "You're a Stewman now. You may be adopted, but so was I. I was born Ryan Russell McCord. The guy who adopted me was adopted, too. And I don't know about the guy who adopted him. But if you look it up, there are not very many Stewmans in existence."

Then I peered deep into his eyes and said, "Son, it's not the name we're given or born with that matters. It's the name that we go out and make for ourselves. I've gone out and made the name Stewman mean something. I've done my best to make this name synonymous with integrity, hard work, discipline, consistency and winning. All I ask is that you do the same. Honor our name because it will get you real influence. It will get you in doors that might otherwise close. You'll have access to people who otherwise may not have been willing to talk to you. It only takes one time to tarnish an entire Wikipedia for a family. Now you have an opportunity to add to it and make it even better."

I wanted my son to know that he wasn't alone. He wasn't the only adopted person, but he already knew that. The bigger lesson I hoped he understood is that none of us know who we are. Many of us don't even keep the name we were born with. I've shown him by example that it's possible to build a name for yourself, no matter what your name is.

As Pastor Keith says, "If you'll give people something to respect and someone to believe in, that combination creates influence." If I carry myself with integrity long enough to be recognized for my integrity in the public eye, people will say, "You can trust this guy." In this state, I suddenly have real influence. As long as I don't start misusing that influence or making bad decisions, I will not be discredited. As long as I remain an example, I will have real influence over people. If I offer them information or something that might help them, they won't be inclined to dismiss it. I have a level of influence as a direct result of my ongoing integrity.

People will believe I am a man of my word because I have given them something to respect. I've explained that integrity means keeping your word. But that's only half of it. Many who aren't respectable keep their word. But if you look at them, you can see they're not physically respectable. They're not mentally respectable. They're not financially respectable.

They think they are the example of integrity based on one factor—their word. It takes more than that to establish integrity.

You have to give people something to respect and believe in. I want people to say, "I respect and believe in Ryan Stewman because he's a man of his word."

**When people respect you and believe
your word, you have true influence.**

I aim to be a respectable, trustworthy person. When I reach that pinnacle, I can sell you anything, anytime, and anywhere. Although, I wouldn't do that because my integrity won't allow me to sell you anything but what I believe in. Still, influence gives you the authority to sell whatever you want. That's because when a person respects you, they believe in you.

Strive to be that person others can believe in and respect, whether that be your spouse, kids, friends, employees, people you work for, your boss, CEO, business partners, in-laws, or anyone else. Give people something to respect—and remember that respect comes from integrity.

When you have influence, suddenly, it's not an ask you're putting out there. It's a pleasure to do business with you. It's not a sale. It's an opportunity for your clients to express that they did business with you. All because you became an example. Your client wants to do business with somebody who's an example of what winning looks like. I want to do business with somebody who's an example of what it's like to make shit happen. I want to do business with somebody who's an example of pure integrity.

As the example, everyone will believe and trust you. If your example is that of respect, belief, honor, integrity, and influence, why wouldn't people believe in and trust you? You are walking the talk every day. You don't have to convince people anymore. I'm not just talking about business, either. You don't have to convince your spouse when you're on the road that you're not in the strip club. You don't have to convince your spouse that you're trustworthy and don't cheat. They don't worry about you because they know you're the example of a great and exceptional partner.

You don't have to convince people that you went to the gym and stuck to your diet this week. They see you are an example of health. The results don't lie.

I was on a coaching call with an elite billionaire. This billionaire said he was very competitive. Then one of the folks on Zoom, who is not a billionaire, said, "I'm more competitive than you." The elite billionaire replied, "Look around. You're not. The results don't lie. I've got billions of them, and you don't. So no, you're not. I hate to put it that way, but you're not." I thought, *man, that's real.*

This man wasn't degrading the other dude. He was just saying, here's the truth–that's integrity. Fake integrity would've been for the elite billionaire to pat that person on the back, saying, "Man, I hope you are. We're going to find out." That's a normal response, but it has no real integrity. The truth was: "No, here's the reality. I've already proved it, and now you'll have to earn it."

This billionaire is an example. He might've blown people's minds with his rough truth, but they all couldn't help but regard him as "That's the example." I know we were all thinking *that's an example of someone I would like to be similar to, or this is someone who has qualities I want to have. They are winning.* Having a real experience like that is why we were on Zoom in the first place.

Keep your word 100% of the time, and no one will doubt you. They'll know your word is as good as gold.

To back up my integrity, I pay fast. We just recently threw an event costing $2 million in speaker fees. We featured Rick Ross, Logan Paul, and David Goggins. It was amazing.

I paid all the speakers before they showed up at the event. I needed everybody to understand that out of integrity and respect, I *wanted* to pay them quickly. As soon as we signed contracts, I sent their money—weeks and even months before the event took place. I paid them in full, which is not typical in our industry. I did that because I wanted to be the example of how I want to be treated—of how everyone should be treated.

That's an example of how easy business with me can be. The next time I call these speakers, they will say with enthusiasm, "Yes, I want to do another deal with you." They'll come back immediately because they know I'm the example of somebody who keeps their word. I'm the example of someone who conducts business the right way. I'm the example of someone they want to work with. That's real influence.

CHAPTER 15

RESPECT IS A GIFT THAT'S EARNED

*"First you get the money,
then you get the power,
then you get the respect."*
—The Lox

We've covered the topic of giving people something to respect. Respect is a common phrase that we use today. Even Cartman from *South Park* will tell you, "Respect my authority!" Here's the disconnect: most people give the word respect lip service. They don't define it, much less understand it.

Let me clarify. Just because we meet, you will not automatically get my respect. You must be a respectable person to earn my respect and that of other people.

You are not entitled to respect. You are not the recipient of a gift of respect. Respect is a gift given to you only when it's earned.

When I meet a person, I judge them on their character, actions, words, and how they carry themselves. There's a difference between a respectable person and one who's not. This is how I classify it: respectful people are polite. As Texans, we say "Yes, ma'am," or "No, ma'am," "Yes, sir," or "No, sir." We say, "Please and thank you." We hold the door open for people. Those are common traits of our respectable culture.

If I'm going to be a respectable Texan and practice the habits of the culture, then I need to hold the doors open for the ladies. I need to hold elevators for approaching people. I need to remember my manners and say, "Yes, sir," or "No, sir," "Yes, ma'am," or "No, ma'am," and "Please and thank you." Acting and speaking in this way as a part of my culture gives me respect among the people around me because they see me giving respect.

At a young age, I learned that I have to give respect to get respect. I can't be a disrespectful motherfucker and expect people to have respect and admiration for me. That equation does not compute. But what does compute is understanding what's respectful and what's not.

When it comes to marriage, what's respectful? Being respectful means showing honor to your spouse. I believe that honor is bigger than love. That was yet another lesson I learned from Pastor Keith—that we touched on in a previous chapter.

Respect and honor run hand in hand. You have to give respect to your spouse to get respect. Allow me to address the male readers for a moment. Most men disrespect their wives. Because they have money, success, or authority, they think their wives must still honor them even as they are dishonoring them. I'm just as guilty as the next person, and I'm not perfect. In my experience, I have seen that happen with men and their marriages, and it's disrespectful.

When you're respectful to your wife and show honor to her, she will respect and honor you in exchange. Often guys wonder why the women in their life don't support them—while at the same time, they're not honoring and respecting them. Remember, respect is a gift. When your spouse gives you the gift of respect, it's earned in increments over time.

This is why we discussed demonstrating consistency in our character and actions. That will earn you respect. Respect isn't just handed out in one lump sum.

For the last 14 years, people have watched me try my best to be and act with integrity to earn their respect. Before that, people watched me fight like hell to do this in real life. I have not earned respect in one fell swoop.

It's not given to me when a person first meets me. I've been at this for 23 fucking years because I know that respect comes in little increments over time. I earned the respect of my friends a hundred times over when they asked me to go party at the strip club and bars, and I told them no each time.

The first time I might have earned a little respect. The second time I might have earned a little more respect. The third time, I know they were thinking, *this guy's got fucking fortitude. He's in. I respect this motherfucker. He is who he says he is.*

As I said, respect is earned in increments over time. There's no shortcut. Even in prison, which is probably the most disrespectful place I've ever been, you have to respect people because if you're disrespectful, they will fight you.

I still have PTSD from being in that place. But it taught me a weird lesson. Even in prison, if you try to shortcut respect, it won't work. You have to be willing to fight for it. That's a metaphor for life. Try to shortcut respect, and you'll have to fight for it. I don't think it's worth fighting to get respect. I was respected in prison, but I didn't have to do a lot of fighting. The second time around, I was still respected, not as a tough guy, but as a smart guy.

**Respect can be earned in different ways.
Bullying creates fear, not respect.**

Respect also has different meanings. Make sure you're on the right side of respect. Respect based on fear is not respect–it's intimidation. You want well-deserved respect, and the only way to get there is to become the example, to live your life as a respectable human being, and as a person who has made the right decisions. It is to continue to make the right decisions so you can hail yourself as respectful.

Before you think I'm on my soapbox and acting as if I've never done anything wrong, let me get straight with you. I'm not going to preach to you and act like I've never fought with my wife, done drugs, or drank too much. I'm not even going to promise those things won't happen in the future. But I'll do my best every day. And more times than not, I do what's respectable.

Even if I am intoxicated, in intense anger, in a spousal fight, or whatever the situation, I still maintain integrity and respect. Shit just might go off the wheels a little bit.

ALL IN, ALL OUT

When it comes to respect, you're either all in or out–there's no halfway to respect. If you're uttering that phrase, it means you don't respect the person you're talking about. It's kind of like what Mobb Deep says, "There's no such thing as halfway crooks." Respect follows that path.

To recap: respect is making the right choices. It's not telling people you made the right choices; it's them *seeing* you make the right choices. They come to respect your decision-making process and wisdom. I've found if people respect your degree of wisdom, they'll respect you in every other area of your life, too.

Our job is to pay due diligence to every facet of the GCode: Gratitude (mental), Genetics (physical), Grind (financial), Group (relationships). Earn respect, and you become the example. People won't respect if you have a bunch of money but are out of shape or if you're in great shape but broke. We're here to have it all.

Remember these high points before you head to the next chapter:

Respect comes in increments over time.

There's no shortcut to respect.

Respect can't be bullied. This isn't the prison yard. This is the path to prosperity.

Respect isn't a gift you're entitled to; you *earn* it one decision at a time.

CHAPTER 16

POWER MOVES

*"Every move you make today should continue
to make moves for you in the future."*

I laid out the path for you to create integrity, influence, and respect. Now it's up to you to do the work.

People in power, whether in the government, Hollywood, or the upper echelon of a company, need to be respectable. People trust them. But as you and I know, very few people are worthy of respect. Some get drunk on power. We've watched individuals representing us in Congress become intoxicated by power. They've passed crazy-ass laws that benefit them but restrain the rest of us. We've watched bureaucrats pass monopoly laws to break up companies so their constituents can make money and build financial empires.

Power runs the world.

Think of the gasoline in your vehicles; that's power.

The electricity in your house; that's power.

The authority in the marketplace; that's power.

The amount of money in a bank account; that's purchasing power.

The amount of strength someone has; that's personal power.

I have promised myself that I will live a powerful life, but let me explain what that is.

To make my point clear, help me out. Take a second and think of the most powerful entity in existence. Really consider it. I ask this question at our live events and seminars. The first reply most people give—and it's a natural response—is God. While it may be true that God is the most powerful entity, we have not seen, felt, or touched God. Many people believe in God's existence, but no scientific proof exists.

I believe the most powerful thing in existence is the sun. The sun's power heats the world here, creating a livable atmosphere for us and every other living thing on this planet. It gives us the ability to prosper and be alive.

The sun photosynthesizes the plants that feed us and many other living things. The sun also keeps other planets in magnetic balance. I have yet to run into anybody who can think of something as powerful as the sun.

When I say power comes in small increments over long periods, consider the power of the sun.

According to what I've read, the sun is 4.6 billion years old. However, the sun was not always the most powerful thing in existence. For a long time, the sun was a solar nebula—a giant spinning cloud of gas and dust that collapsed under its gravity until it became the yellow dwarf star it is today. This event heated the sun to make it a raging fireball. It has burned for billions of years and will continue to burn for billions of years until it burns out.[10]

I mention the sun because I believe everything in nature has a supernatural correlation. That's a blueprint for how we can gain power.

For long periods, power goes unrecognized. For billions of years, the sun wasn't shit. It wasn't hot. It was cold—like our lives!

---

[10] https://solarsystem.nasa.gov/solar-system/sun/in-depth/

For decades, you're cold, and no one notices you even though you're making responsible and respectable decisions. But then you keep at it, and the next thing you know, the world is paying attention to you. The world sees that you've got a history of making good decisions.

Now, boom, you're powerful. This is where the supernatural part comes into play.

What no one sees, God sees.

When your friends don't see, God sees.

When your spouse doesn't see, God sees.

Not Santa Claus, not the Easter Bunny, the Almighty God sees how you are when you're with people. He sees how you are when you're alone.

I'm friends with many pastors, but who I am doesn't change depending on the company I'm keeping. I'm the same Ryan Stewman, whether I'm with Pastor Keith Craft or someone fresh out of prison with gang tattoos all over him. It doesn't matter. I don't change. When Keith or Erwin McManus show up, and I'm telling a dirty joke, I'm telling a dirty joke. They better listen in or walk away because I'm not changing.

But most people in the middle of telling a dirty joke when the preacher walks up will say, "Oh, hey, it's the preacher. We were just sitting here about to pray. You want to join in and pray with us?" They alter who they are.

They put on a façade. I don't think it matters if people adjust what they're saying in front of a preacher. God, the Universe, or whatever higher power you believe in, always watches you anyway. It knows whether you're truly a person worthy of power.

UN-TRASHING THE PLACE

I tell this next story about myself not to pat myself on the back but to share my experience so you can understand how much life experiences have shaped my perspective.

When I enter my office building and use the restroom, I clean it up if it needs it. If there are napkins or trash on the floor, I put them in the waste basket. If the sink is wet, I wipe it down. I don't grouch about it. I don't say anything to anybody. I wipe down what needs it, pick up the garbage, and throw it away.

If a light's on, I turn it off.

If I get out of a chair, I push it up to the table.

If I turn on the water, I do so just long enough for me to use it.

I try not to waste anything and leave this place better than I found it.

I don't do this to say, "Hey, hey, hey, look at me. I'm picking up trash." I just throw it away because I have this theory that God's watching. It's not in the Bible or any religious books. It's just me wondering, *what if God's up there watching, and every time I walked by a piece of trash and didn't pick it up, God said, 'I gave him an opportunity to be great, and he passed it?'* *What if every time I walked by a piece of trash, God said, 'I gave him an opportunity to make the world a better place, and he decided not to?'* *What if every time I left my chair out, God said, 'I gave him an opportunity to show that he understood the purpose of order in his life, but he doesn't?'*

**I believe God has a point system that has everything
to do with how we act when no one's looking.**

When I got out of prison the first time, I told myself *I'm not going to do anything in the dark that I wouldn't do in the light.* There's nothing I won't do or say that I wouldn't do in front of a preacher or the president of the United States.

That's how I hold myself accountable. So in public, I pick up trash, and in secret, I pick up trash. I don't need to remind anybody or tell anybody what I did, but I hope that I'm making God, the Universe, or whatever you want to believe in, happy as It looks down on me. I hope God sees that everywhere I go, even when people aren't paying attention, I'm paying attention and trying to leave this world a better place. I'm trying to clean up people's minds. I'm trying to clean up people's lives. And I'm trying to clean up this planet by doing the little bit I can. Maybe I'm only picking up one piece of trash a day. Maybe I'm only picking up one bottle on the ground. Maybe I'm only picking up a few napkins, but that's a few more than everybody else.

Maybe I'm the only one returning my shopping cart each time I use it. By doing so, I believe I set an example. Maybe I not only put my shopping cart up, but I grabbed yours, too, because you left yours out—another example of my resolve. I've kept that mindset for the last 23 years of my life. And I believe that mindset and the actions that come with it, bit by bit, little by little, have led me to be a powerful influence on others.

I am not a leader of countries, cities, or states. I just run businesses. But I couldn't run successful businesses or manage and lead people without my belief in and adherence to the point system.

Lest you think I am just blowing up my points, I also subtract them. I lose my shit. I talk bad to somebody. I have an angry moment here and there; that's my downfall. But every day, I'm scoring more than I'm deducting.

When I get to Heaven, the pearly gates, or whatever you believe in, I want to be able to say, "I did my best. I was not perfect, but I did my best to always improve myself, those around me, and my environment." I want to be able to say, "I tried my best to be an example."

Let me ask you again, "Will you try your best to become an example?" God needs more people. And that point system will get you there!

CHAPTER 17

YOUR ELITE FUTURE

*"You know who you are capable of being.
Excuses are thieves of your greatness."*

Once you understand the responsibility, influence, and power that comes with being an example, you will experience a lot of pushback from the force of average. It will give you excuses.

Here's a classic: "I've been good for X amount of time. I deserve to slip once." It's what people say to themselves when they're on a diet and need a cheat day. "I've been good for six days. I need a cheat day."

As you go forward to become the greatest version of yourself, I can't say it enough: the force of average will challenge you. That's why very few examples of people in their most elite version exist. Not many people can truly say they are an example of what winning looks like at all times. Too many people fall victim to the force of average. You may be 30, 40, or 50 years old reading this book. The force of average has been around for centuries, if not a millennium.

When you feel like you're going to tap out and quit, remember FYE, Fuck Your Excuses—all you have to do is hold those three little letters in your mind at all times.

**When you think you've got a legit reason to stop,
don't forget that's synonymous with failure.**

You need a strong weapon against the force of average. Otherwise, it's going to feed you reasons to fail. It's going to tell you're not a respectable person. It's going to tell you, in the words of Kanye West, "No one man should have all that power."

But we deserve it.

Barrel through the barricades and roadblocks that block you from greatness. Excuses are landmines in the field you're trying to cross to get to safety on the other side. Excuses are enemy fire at the greatest version of yourself.

Get into an adamant mindset that your excuses are not for sale, bargaining, or negotiation. And they're damn sure not for you.

You have to carry yourself knowing that you're the example, people look up to you, and you have influence and power.

No excuse allows you to be on for six days and off for one. I could be an example of a good husband for six days, but on the seventh day, cheat and beat. I could be an example of a person in great physical shape for six days, but on the seventh day, do a whole bunch of drugs and alcohol and eat like shit all day long. Achieving greatness doesn't work that way.

You're either all in or all out. Even one day a week is out. I can't one day per week decide to be a shitty husband. I can't one day per week decide not to run companies. I can't one day per week decide I'm not the CEO; now, I'm a bum. I can't one day per week decide I'm not a father.

I don't get a day off from greatness. I don't get a day off from being the example. I have to be on at all times. That's why so many weak motherfuckers will never even step up to the plate to try to be the example. They know how hard it is, and they strike out.

But you're not like that. You made it through this book. That means you want to move into the greatest version of yourself—the example you know you can be.

You have a desire to find out what that's like.

Or maybe you've always felt a hunch that you can become the example.

That's why you're still reading all these pages later.

Knowing this, you need to carry yourself with the FYE mentality. I have it tattooed on my hand. Many of my friends, clients, coworkers, employees, and partners have it tattooed somewhere on them. We carry ourselves knowing we're the example, whether anybody on Earth is looking or not. That doesn't matter because we know God's looking, and the Universe is looking.

My ultimate physical goal on this planet is to stay frozen in time while I advance my body and spirit. I want to be an example like my pastor, Keith Craft. At 63 years old, that guy looks no older than 40. He is still jacked. Keith is a lot taller and bigger than I am, but you get the point of how I want to appear in my sixties.

Pastor Keith is still advancing. He's still reading. He's still learning. He's still gaining wisdom. He's still growing. That's what I want to do. He's the example I look up to as the example I want to set.

This is contagion.

I want my body to remain in the state where it is right now, and I'm willing to put in the work for it. I'm willing to continue to advance in my mind and spirit, to give more in every area of my life, including my time, talent, treasure, church, and charities. I will grow through reading and learning more and through voraciously seeking wisdom.

I intend to improve myself through books, programs, and mentors because I'm on a path to becoming the most elite version of myself.

I don't get any days off.

Failure's not an option.

My mission in life is to help as many people as possible become the greatest version of themselves. That means I must become the greatest version of myself first. I'm on the path.

Every day, I improve a little bit.

Every day, I get a little better.

Every day, I get a little bit smarter.

Every day, I get a little bit stronger.

The more I grow and develop, the more I can support those around me to do the same. That's a failsafe.

The greatness within me inspires greatness in others.

Part of my path on this planet is to become a greatness extractor. I can only extract greatness from others if I show them it's within me.

When you compare my past life to now, you see a guy working on greatness. I am working on me for me, yes, but I want to inspire you to be the greatest, too. I can't fail at that mission. I'm committed to it for 48 hours a day and seven days a week for the rest of my life. I decided to become an example forever. I'm hoping that after you finish this book, you'll make that decision, too.

The world needs more of us. The world needs people who are respectable and that others can believe in but not as deities or false idols. We need to see people's achievements that will encourage us to think *that guy's a winner. I trust him. I believe in him. I'll cheer him on.* Or *she's a winner and an amazing human. I believe in her. I'll cheer her on. She's an example of what I want my daughter to be. He's an example of what I want my son to be. They are an example of what I want our marriage to be.*

The example shows the world what winning looks like at all times.

I often tell my employees and clients, when you go to the airport, I better not see you wearing sweats with your hair all disheveled.

Winners don't look like that. Winners represent winning at all times.

When you go through the airport, you better be in peak shape. Be alert. Be well put together. You never know who's going to walk up to you, take a picture or video of you—and now, *you're on social media.* There's no escaping from reality.

We represent what winning looks like at all times. As examples, that's what we have to do. We don't act crazy, mouth off, or lose our temper.

We do respectable things repeatedly over long periods because that's what it takes to win in life. That's what it takes to gather power in life.

More importantly, this isn't about tooting your own horn. This is about living life and operating as the best version of yourself. It is about being so extreme that other people say, "Look at him. He's an example." Or, "Look at her. She's an example."

I'm calling on you from the bottom of my heart, and with everything I have, to become the example. The world needs you. It needs you to represent what winning looks like at all times so you can show young boys and girls what is possible and old men and women what is still attainable.

Be the example.

AFTERWORD

Ryan Stewman is an example of an awesome father; you can tell by the way his kids admire him.

Ryan Stewman is an example of an amazing husband; you can tell by the way his wife looks at him.

Ryan Stewman is an example of an inspirational leader; you can tell by the way his staff looks up to him.

Ryan Stewman is an example of a spiritual man; you can tell by the way pastors are always with him.

Ryan Stewman is an example of a social media star; you can tell by the way his competitors watch him.

Ryan Stewman is an example of a serial entrepreneur; you can tell by the way the press talks about him.

Dan Fleyshman
Founder, Model Citizen Fund

WHY JOIN APEX?

If you're ready to be the example for your friends, family, and business, then you should join Apex Entourage. What is Apex? It's a network, mastermind, coaching, and training program that helps you become the most elite version of yourself. Even more than that, it's a group of people who represent what winning looks like at all times.

Apex members include doctors, lawyers, influencers, construction workers, plumbers, and more people from all walks of life and industries. It isn't the Ryan Stewman show, either. I'm a member just like anyone else, and I share my exceptional value with the group just like everyone else.

Apex members:

- Speak on stages
- Have verified social media profiles
- Build real and highly profitable businesses
- Plus so much more.

Apex is for anyone who wants to win. We will teach you how, but not only that...

Apex teaches you:

- How to win in your health
- How to win in your finances
- How to win investing
- How to win in relationships
- How to win as a leader
- And obviously, how to become an example for everyone around you

That's what separates Apex Entourage from other masterminds and groups. You'll not only receive the tools to create a beast of a sales machine for your business but you will be given the tools to unlock the greatness that's already within you so you can enjoy success in all areas of your life—not just your business.

Apex means "the top." That's what this program is—a clear path to the top of your game.

There are three levels:

1. Entourage
2. Entrepreneurs
3. Executives

This gives you a starting point no matter where you are in the game of life.

Since you've read this book, I already know your mind is in the right place to become the example for those around you as well as for your business. I'd like to align with you and help you become the very best at what you do, no matter what that might be.

When you're ready to take the next step to become your greatest self, I'll see you on this page:

www.JoinTheApex.com

Thank you for reading. I can't wait to help you.

ABOUT THE AUTHOR

Ryan Stewman started his journey of becoming one of the world's most prolific sales trainers and speakers when he was a salesman. In a few short years, he became a CEO and is now not only an entrepreneur, but he's an investor with over 60+ companies in his portfolio.

His wasn't always a smooth road. A rough upbringing and multiple tragic setbacks early in life left him penniless and homeless multiple times. Ryan had no head start and no help while on his journey to the top.

What does he credit his meteoric rise to success to? Simply: doing the work. Thanks to his no-BS approach to strategizing and scaling businesses, he's helped over 20-25K high net worth clients adjust their business plans resulting in windfall profits as they became the most elite versions of themselves.

Ryan has amassed a social following of over four million people; he's been featured regularly in *Forbes, Entrepreneur, HuffPost,* and many other massive publications. He is a best-selling author with more than 13 books to his name and is also the sitting CEO of nine different multi-million-dollar companies, including Phonesites.com, Break Free Academy, and Wolfeman Assets.

When he's not dominating his industry and setting the example for other high-level entrepreneurs and his team, he's at his home in Dallas, TX, setting the example for the ones he loves most.

Alongside his gorgeous wife, Amy, he's a doting father to his three boys, Jax, Asher, and Colton, and the newest family addition, his daughter, Harlyn, who is the spitting image of Amy.

Despite his struggles, Ryan's climb to success continues. He will continue to provide value to people around the world for as long as possible.

DISCLAIMER

The advice and events outlined in this book are for informational purposes only. The lessons and the ways in which you can become the example for the people in your life are just my opinion. It's worked for me, so I wanted to share it with you, but I could be full of shit, too. So read and act on this advice at your own risk. But like I said, it worked for me, and if it worked for me, it could work for you. That's why I wrote it.

The results of taking the actions outlined in this book may vary, and the editors and I make no guarantees regarding the results. So don't try to sue me or anyone else associated with this book.

Made in United States
North Haven, CT
25 October 2022

25912921R00080